Time We Started Listening

Duncan Reid

Time We Started Listening

Theological Questions put to us by Recent Indigenous Writing

Duncan Reid

ATF Theology
Adelaide
2020

A Forum for Theology in the World
Volume 7, Issue 2, 2020

A Forum for Theology in the World is an academic refereed journal aimed at engaging with issues in the contemporary world, a world which is pluralist and ecumenical in nature. The journal reflects this pluralism and ecumenism. Each edition is theme specific and has its own editor responsible for the production. The journal aims to elicit and encourage dialogue on topics and issues in contemporary society and within a variety of religious traditions. The Editor in Chief welcomes submissions of manuscripts, collections of articles, for review from individuals or institutions, which may be from seminars or conferences or written specifically for the journal. An internal peer review is expected before submitting the manuscript. It is the expectation of the publisher that, once a manuscript has been accepted for publication, it will be submitted according to the house style to be found at the back of this volume. All submissions to the Editor in Chief are to be sent to: hdregan@atf.org.au.

Each edition is available as a journal subscription, or as a book in print, pdf or epub, through the ATF Press web site — www.atfpress.com. Journal subscriptions are also available through EBSCO and other library suppliers.

Art work 'Mighty River Red Gums, Echuca', painted by Judy Talacko c 1968, used with permission
Cover design Myf Cadwallader

Editor in Chief
Hilary Regan, ATF Press

A Forum for Theology in the World is published by ATF Theology and imprint of ATF (Australia) Ltd
(ABN 90 116 359 963) and
is published twice or three times a year.

ISBN: 978-1-925679-80-9 soft
         978-1-925679-81-6 hard
         978-1-925679-82-3 epub
         978-1-925679-83-0 pdf

Published by:

An imprint of the ATF Press Publishing
Group owned by ATF (Australia) Ltd.
PO Box 234
Brompton, SA 5007
Australia
ABN 90 116 359 963
www.atfpress.com
Making a lasting impact

This little book is for you:
Isaac and Stacey, Nathanael and Holly, Hannah and Cal,
and for Oscar
and your friends, siblings, and cousins,
in the hope that you will live in a more reconciled country,
a more complete commonwealth.

A Forum for Theology in the World Vol 7 No 2/2020

Table of Contents

Foreword

What distinguishes white theology from Indigenous theology? This is not as straightforward a question as it might appear. Take the term' white', for starters. What, or who, is 'white'? In common parlance, 'white people' (meaning people with pale skin) are routinely distinguished from 'black', 'brown', 'red' or 'yellow' people. Of course, it is often said that 'white' people invented the categories, but that is not quite true. In fact, the people who invented the categories described themselves simply as 'people', with no qualifying adjective. For they saw themselves as the paradigmatic model, and everyone else as just a little deficient, somehow. Later on, when those of us deemed 'deficient' learned to play this game, we started to call the game-makers 'white', which was both a clever move and a stupid move, at the same time. It was clever because it brought into focus the hitherto repressed fact that human beings participate equally in the ontological quality of humanness whatever subsequent qualifiers one might then apply, whether that be skin colour, ethnicity, gender, or whatever. It was stupid, however, at the very same time, because by playing the game in this way we who were hitherto 'deficient' conceded the game. We conceded, that is, that both the game and its most basic rules were legitimate. We found ourselves, therefore, in an ethical double-bind: play the game, but by no means play the game.

A similar dynamic is at play in the word 'theology'. Those who invented the word were apparently residents of Athens in the fourth century of the 'common era' (itself a problematic notion which I cannot address here). It was a term that found its way into Jewish and Christian thinking because of the colonisation of multiple regions and peoples—including Galilee and Judea—by the Greek empires of subsequent centuries. Following the destruction of the temple at

Jerusalem in 70 CE, the *lingua franca* of Jewish and then Christian diasporas was Greek for many centuries: more permanently, of course, in the Eastern Roman Empire than in the West. But the Western (or Latin) forms, which came to dominate European Christianity from at least the 6th century CE, remained essentially Greek in character. Theology, as an intellectual discipline, might therefore be understood as a language game that is essentially colonial: an absorption and modification of first century events and stories from Roman-occupied Galilee and Judea into a larger Hellenistic imagination. This leaves all Christians, even the few who remain in Galilee and Palestine to this day, with an unavoidable paradox: that the Jewish, Aramaic-speaking, Jesus and his followers can only be encountered in their Greek versions. Which is to say, that the only Jesus we have is already a colonised Jesus. He is a 'Jew-Greek' hybrid. He is, as Derrida would say, onto-theological. Colonised by empire.

Thankfully the repressed is never entirely erased, and those rendered 'deficient' still have some agency. The crucified and risen Jesus was able to escape his colonial bonds and inspire multiple movements of liberation and release. Here in the lands now called 'Australia', Indigenous people are rising up to claim what has been repressed, destroyed or stolen: country, kin, dreamings. In doing so, some of us are claiming Jesus as an ally. For the colonised Jesus who, in the hands of missionaries and colonial gubbas alike, became a whip to keep us down, is also a gift from our creator-ancestors, a gift which can be deployed against our captors. In our hands, the Greek Jesus can become Jewish again by first becoming Indigenous. For he is like us, and we are like him. Together we belong to the great company of 'deficients' imprinted with his paschal story:

> We are afflicted in every way, but not crushed;
> perplexed, but not driven to despair;
> persecuted, but not forsaken;
> struck down, but not destroyed;
> always carrying in the body the death of Jesus,
> so that the life of Jesus may also be made visible in our bodies.
>
> 2 Corinthians 4:8–10

This tiny example of Indigenous theologising reveals, I hope, two things. First, that Aboriginal and Torres Strait Islander peoples will never entirely escape the fact that we are a colonised people. I write in an Indo-European language. I am educated in European intellectual traditions. I am as much Irish and British as I am Aboriginal. I am a Christian. But the second thing my theologising reveals, I hope, is that I have not entirely lost my Trawloolway identity and responsibility to country. I am seeking to re-read, to re-interpret, to re-imagine as much of the colonial inheritance as I can within that frame, for the sake of my people, and for the sake of our captors. For our colonial overlords are as much the victims of their Greek thinking as we are.

I am privileged to be alive in an era when a small handful of Euro-Australian theologians have decided to re-evaluate their faith through the eyes of First Peoples. Some of you will know their names: John Harris, Rob Bos, Norman Habel, Mark Brett, Chris Budden, Grant Finlay. To that very short list may now be added the name of Duncan Reid. In what follows, Duncan listens to what we are saying, treats what we are saying seriously, and seeks to articulate some measure of understanding. He is motivated, it seems, by a profound sense of crisis around the impotence of European theological traditions in the face of genocide and, especially, our global environmental catastrophe. I congratulate Duncan for this beginning (for that is what it is) and encourage both him and his readers to stay the course into deeper and yet more challenging waters.

Garry Worete Deverell
Poorneet (Tadpole Season)
Nairm (Melbourne)

Acknowledgements

Some years ago in Canberra, a colleague who I've known since the 1970s, asked if I still had a book in me, wanting to get out. My reply at that stage was: no, probably not. But then along came the global pandemic, which gave me some extra free time for reading, writing and reflecting over several months, during which time I realised I did in fact have something I needed to say, and say as a matter of urgency. So this is an iso-book, written during the isolation lock-down, when libraries were closed and conversations with friends and colleagues somewhat curtailed. It was written without access to some of the texts I'd like to have consulted, or revisited. I was dependent on what I had immediately available to me, including the often incomplete notes on books I'd read previously. But the sense of urgency prevailed over my customary sense of caution: I needed to draw attention to some things that I feel we, all of us, need to listen to.

I need to thank several people who were willing to talk about these issues and read this essay in an draft form: Revd Dr Sandy Yule, who encouraged me to tell more of my own story in this narrative, and to pursue the distinction between connected and disconnected people; Dr Bronwyn Stokes, who has lived in the Kimberley and speaks Nyikina; to Revd Dr Garry Worete Deverell and Revd Glenn Loughrey, two Indigenous colleagues who both offered valuable correctives from their own perspectives on what I'd written, and what I'd failed to see and hear in their own writings. Thank you to my niece Eva Parton, who has lived in Arnhem Land and speaks Yolgnu, for conversations; to my brother-in-law Peter Horne, for sharing his understanding of the management thinking in the mining industry; to my colleague Revd Helen Creed who read and commented on a near-final version of the draft and to my former theological student,

Rt Revd Jeremy Greaves, who read through the final version; and to Professor Mark Brett (whom I consulted far too late for any substantive improvements to this text) and to Mr Chris Chant, Principal of Caulfield Junior College, who shared photos of the William Dargie murals there. Thank you to Judy Talacko for her kind permission to use her very evocative painting of river red gums for the cover of this book, and to Myf Cadwallader, who worked this painting into the cover design. I am grateful to my colleagues at Camberwell Girls Grammar School, who, during the first stage of the 2020 lockdown cancelled some of my classes, with the effect of allowing me time to read and write, and the school librarians there who were very willing to buy recent works by Indigenous writers. Thank you to all my students, past and present: you have taught me, and continue to teach me far more than you might ever imagine. I am especially grateful to Murrundindi, Ngurungaeta of the Wurundjeri people, on whose traditional country this essay was written, for ongoing conversations and for agreeing to read and comment on earlier and later versions of this text. Thank you to Hilary Regan from ATF Press, who was willing to publish these thoughts. Thank you, Fiona, for encouraging my curiosity in exploring this topic and supporting me in my reading and writing around this complex of issues.

Duncan Reid
All Saints' Day, 2020

Approaches to Indigenous Cultures

Background

Until recently it was problematic in Australia for a non-Indigenous person, such as me, to comment on Indigenous writings. I remember twenty-five years ago being advised (though not by an Indigenous person) against venturing into this territory, even to offer a response. Australia was and still is emerging from more than two centuries of non-Indigenous people determining what was best (and very often delivering what was worst[1]), in our understandings, for Indigenous people. William Russell puts the matter with blunt honesty: 'They've spent generations telling us what to be and think.'[2] The corrective to this was long overdue. It was a corrective that could hardly come from non-Indigenous voices, as Sarah Maddison has argued.[3] Tyson Yunkaporta expresses this point when he warns that 'making yourself an expert in another culture is not always appreciated by the members of that culture. Understanding your own culture and the way it interacts with others, particularly the power dynamics of it,

---

1. Bruce Elder, *Blood on the Wattle: Massacres and Maltreatment of Australian Aborigines since 1788* (Sydney: Child & Associates, 1988) opened up a discussion that had previously been largely taboo in Australia, but which is now the subject of a major research project led by Lyndall Ryan at the University of Newcastle, see: <https://c21ch.newcastle.edu.au/colonialmassacres/> (accessed 4 April 2020).
2. William Russell, 'A story from my life,' in *Growing up Aboriginal in Australia*, edited by Anita Heiss (Melbourne: Black Inc, 2018), 203–10, here at 204.
3. Sarah Maddison, *The Colonial Fantasy: Why White Australia Can't Solve Back Problems* (Sydney: Allen & Unwin, 2019).

is far more appreciated.'[4] This is a call to understand the problematic of the dominant western culture in Australia vis-à-vis Indigenous cultures. Elsewhere Yunkaporta asserts:

> Strong Indigenous voices need to be doing more than recounting our subjective experiences—we also need to be examining the narratives of the occupying culture and challenging them with counter-narratives . . .. We should examine the history of this civilisation . . . very closely.[5]

Indigenous voices have become more confident, demanding and controlling respect in ways that were not possible even twenty-five years ago. The amount and scope of Indigenous writing in the past two decades is remarkable; even more remarkable are the insights that have emerged within this writing, and the growing strength of Indigenous voices in Australian social and political life. Even so, I am aware of the danger identified by Jack Latimore of groups (or indeed individuals like myself) 'aligning Indigenous interests with their own'.[6] This is very far from my intention—though, in view of the history of the activities of various churches in relation to Aboriginal people, I can understand scepticism about such a claim.

A few things about myself. My people came here (yes, on those tall ships) from Perthshire and Caithness in central and north-eastern Scotland, from Devon in the south-west of England, and from County Cork in south-west Ireland. I realise I have spent much of my life unwittingly taking Tyson Yunkaporta's advice about examining my own culture and 'the way it interacts with others.' I spent four years exploring the language and storytelling of the English-speaking peoples, from Caedmon onwards. I've read Stuart Macintyre and Anna Clark's *History Wars*,[7] and a fair bit (admittedly not all) of

---

4. Tyson Yunkaporta, *Sand Talk: How Indigenous Thinking Can Save the World* (Melbourne: Text, 2019), 97.

5. Yunkaporta, *Sand Talk*, 133. This is not to say listening to the subjective experiences of Indigenous people is unimportant. See Heiss *Growing up Aboriginal in Australia*.

6. Jack Latimore. 'Far enough away to be on my way back home,' in Heiss, *Growing up Aboriginal*, 138–46, here at 145.

7. Stuart Macintyre and Anna Clark, *The History Wars* (Melbourne: Melbourne University Press, 2003).

Manning Clark's *History of Australia*.[8] More central to my personal sense of identity, however, is my worldview, which is Christian, with an Anglican cultural flavour. I have spent more years than I like to admit examining this culture very closely, trying to fathom the deep significance of some of Christianity's most puzzling claims. As an ordained office holder, I am recognised within my church community as a custodian of these traditions.

The thinking for this essay began many years ago, going back ultimately to the family home in which I grew up. My mother's uncle, Bert Warren, had led the 1933 Peace Expedition to negotiate with local people of Caledon Bay, after the killings of five Japanese fishermen. Prior to that, the standard government response would have been a punitive expedition by armed police. Although I never knew my great-uncle, his memory, and a clutch of Arnhem Land artefacts, were presences in our family home. The artefacts, a rather tattered but well-used pandanus grass sewing basket, a baobab seed decorated with x-ray vision kangaroos, goannas and emus (until it happened to be dropped and broken—these things were never kept behind glass, they were always just there, lying around), and a couple of far more sturdy waddies. The house itself had an Arnhem Land name. I remember my Mum telling me that when they were approached by the Caledon Bay locals on the beach, the four-man peace expedition had thought they were unarmed, until they were close enough to see they were all cleverly carrying very long spears between their toes. With the benefit of hindsight, of course, we could ask: what were Japanese fishermen doing on the remote northern coast of Australia, anyway, in the early 1930s? My sister and I were also made aware very early of the story's tragic and shameful ending: Dagiar, the Caledon Bay man who was persuaded to go to Darwin to stand trial, was imprisoned for four months, convicted and sentenced to death, then acquitted on appeal—all this among people with whom he had no common language. He subsequently 'disappeared' and never returned to his family and home country.[9] This memory of living with

---

8. CMH Clark, *A History of Australia*, volumes I–VI (Melbourne: Melbourne University Press, 1963ff.)

9. The story of these events is told in Keith Cole, *Groote Eylandt Pioneer: A Biography of the Reverend Hubert Ernest de Mey Warren, Pioneer missionary and explorer among the Aborigines of Arnhem Land* (Melbourne: Church Missionary Historical Publications, 1971), 84–101; and John Harris, *We Wish We'd Done More: Ninety Years of CMS and Aboriginal Issues in North Australia*, revised edition (Adelaide: Openbook, 1998), 231–56.

Aboriginal people was not only in my mother's family; my father's grandmother, Jessie Craig, who was born in Melbourne in 1845, had as a child been given an Aboriginal name by the people among whom her Scottish family lived in western Victoria.[10] I also remember, as a teenager in the 1960s and at the encouragement of my Mum's brother, reading Nene Gare's *The Fringe Dwellers*, and the sense of deep disquiet it provoked.[11] But this essay was also prompted by more recent experiences, including the privilege of ongoing conversations with several Aboriginal people, both in South Australia and Victoria. Another was two conversations with theological colleagues who encouraged me to write something about the theological content in recent Australian literature, and especially for some theological thinking from Australia that may be of interest beyond this country. This essay does not claim to be an attempt at Australian Indigenous theology—that is a task for Indigenous theologians. Rather, it is a response from a non-Indigenous Australian theological perspective, to recent Australian Indigenous writings.

I am coming to this conversation, then, from a background of trying to understand my own non-Indigenous culture, and to know the worldview of my own ancestors, both genetic and spiritual, and to bring this complex sense of identity into conversation with this country on which I live. I was born on and live on Wurundjeri land, and I value the various welcomes I have received to this country. I have also lived more than a decade on Kaurna land, and have been welcomed to that country, as well as to Ngarrindjeri country. This is why I want to listen to what Yunkaporta calls the 'yarns,' the stories that reflect Indigenous experience in Australia. And to this conversation I would like to bring a bit of a yarn of my own. A yarn is a two-way and generally rather roundabout sort of exchange. One thing that Indigenous (and some non-Indigenous) writers are fairly consistent in asking of us non-Indigenous Australians is that we *listen* to what Indigenous people have to say, to what their traditions have

---

10. I'm uncertain which Aboriginal group this would have been, but probably either Djargurdwurrung or Giraiwurung. The story is told in Alexander Henderson, *Early Pioneer Families of Victoria and Riverina* (Melbourne: McCarron, Bird & Co, 1935), 323.
11. Nene Gare, *The Fringe Dwellers* (Melbourne: Heinemann, 1961).

to say, and above all, to listen to country.[12] This is my intention here. I am very much heartened by Tyson Yunkaporta's remark that 'you don't need to be an expert to understand the knowledge processes of people from other cultures and enter into dialogues with them'.[13]

So I am now going to venture into this territory. I note also the extraordinary hospitality of Australian Aboriginal people toward outsiders, a hospitality and generosity noted by Tony Swain in the title (and substance) of his book *A Place for Strangers*,[14] and in different contexts by Ros Moriarty,[15] Mark McKenna,[16] and Bruce Pascoe, when he offers: 'The riches of the oldest human culture on earth are available to Australians; very little of it is prohibited to the uninitiated or to those of a different race'.[17] This essay is a small attempt to respond to this hospitality and generosity. I hope it may become a contribution to mutual understanding; a small attempt, as well, at paying—in the best way I can do it—just a bit the unpaid rent mentioned in John Batman's treaty with the Wurundjeri. I am aware that this is not yet the deep listening to country in all its complexity that Indigenous thinkers call for, but rather a sort of preparatory listening, to the voices of some of those Indigenous thinkers as they talk about deep listening.[18] I begin with the disclaimer that my understanding of these voices may be way off the mark. To paraphrase St Augustine,

12. Ros Moriarty, *Listening to Country: A Journey to the Heart of What it Means to Belong* (Sydney: Allen & Unwin, 2011). The recent studies by Bruce Pascoe (*Dark Emu: Aboriginal Australia and the Birth of Agriculture* [Broome: Magabala Books, 2018]), Tyson Yunkaporta (*Sand Talk*), and Victor Steffensen (*Fire Country* [Melbourne: Hardie Grant, 2020]), are all written in the hope that non-Indigenous Australians will finally start to listen. To these we should add the recent range of Indigenous novel-writing and storytelling.
13. Yunkaporta, *Sand Talk*, 97.
14. Tony Swain, *A Place for Strangers: Towards a History of Australian Aboriginal Being* (Cambridge: Cambridge University Press, 1993).
15. Moriarty, *Listening to Country*, 109.
16. Mark McKenna, *Moment of Truth: Quarterly Essay 69* (Melbourne: Black Inc, 2018), 65.
17. Bruce Pascoe, 'Sea Wolves,' in *Salt: Selected Stories and Essays* (Melbourne: Black Inc, 2019), 106–15, here at 115.
18. Glenn Loughrey, *On Being Blackfella's Young Fella: Is Being Aboriginal Enough?* (Melbourne: Coventry, 2020), 133–35.

I'm not sure quite how to say some of this stuff, but think it's better to say something than say nothing.[19]

In this essay I use the terms Indigenous or Aboriginal Australian to refer to First Peoples in Australia; and non-Indigenous Australian, or Second Peoples, to refer to immigrants of the past 230 or so years and their descendants. Even this distinction, however, is problematic as most Aboriginal people now have some immigrant ancestry, and sometimes 'immigrants' find, often to their surprise, an Aboriginal component in their own ancestry.[20] Perhaps in part because of this complexity, Yunkaporta offers a generous definition of Indigenous, when he writes:

> For the purposes of the thought experiments on sustainability in this book, an Indigenous person is a member of a community retaining memories of life lived sustainably on a land-base, as part of that land-base. Indigenous Knowledge is any application of those memories as living knowledge to improve present and future circumstances.[21]

Victor Steffensen is similarly inclusive in his reflections on conversations with Indigenous people in Finland and North America, preferring a term free of any suggestions of ethnicity: 'connected' (to country and heritage), as opposed to 'disconnected' from these things.[22] When I refer to Indigenous writers I simply mean writers who explicitly claim Australian Aboriginal heritage (under Australian law such claims also have to be acknowledged and accepted as genuine by a particular Indigenous group[23]). Writers who make no such explicit claim to indigeneity I assume to be non-Indigenous.

---

19. Augustine, *De Trinitate*, V, 9: '*Dictum est tamen . . . non ut illud diceretur sed ne taceretur.*' <https://www.thelatinlibrary.com/augustine/trin5.shtml> (accessed 18 September 2020).
20. Bruce Pascoe, Rearranging the Dead Cat,' in *Salt*, 89–100, here at 98. See also the discussion of this problem by Stan Grant, *On Identity* (Melbourne: Melbourne University Press, 2019).
21. Yunkaporta, *Sand Talk*, 42.
22. Steffensen, *Fire Country*, 117–8.
23. See Stan Grant, *Talking to My Country* (Sydney: HarperCollins, 2017), 3, for definitions of indigeneity. I have chosen not to identify particular nation or language group identities of the writers here, unless they seem important to the substance of the writing.

Why a theological response?

My own way of listening and entering into dialogue is to bring what I hear into conversation with my own theological worldview and my own religious and cultural traditions, generally in writing. For me to reflect theologically is my way of taking with utter seriousness what Indigenous Australians are saying to Australia and more generally to the world. This is also appropriate as a starting point, according to a significant theological interpreter of cultures, Kathryn Tanner: 'Where one starts in these processes (i.e. of theological interpretation) is literally a matter of where one is concretely—socially, politically, practically. It is a matter of one's very particular historical and social locations . . ..'[24]

Several of the authors considered here insist that there is no longer any pure indigeneity in Australia: Indigenous people live and practise culture in a western cultural context. It also needs to be said that there is no pure gospel unaffected by culture. In fact, gospel is conveyed by culture, as Christianity has always conceded in its practice of translating the words of Jesus, and later the scriptures, from the original languages. The gospel is embedded in cultural forms, and this is for a good theological reason: the incarnation was embedded in a particular culture, at a particular time and place. The incarnate one might have opposed certain aspects of the culture of his day but was not and could not be immune to or untouched by that culture. An example of this is the story of the Syrophoenician (Mk 7:24–30) or Canaanite (Matt 15:21–28) woman, in which Jesus displays the typical prejudices of his day (about women, and Indigenous people), but is persuaded to change his mind.[25] He had to speak the language of his own place and people, in his own mother-tongue, and live— most of the time—by the same cultural norms.

There is then a dialectical relationship between gospel and culture, and it is inevitable that some aspects of culture will be subject to critique from the gospel. In the same way, some aspects of how the gospel is conveyed and certain actions supposedly inspired by the gospel will

---

24. Kathryn Tanner, *Theories of Culture: A New Agenda for Theology* (Minneapolis: Fortress, 1997), 88.
25. See Garry Worete Deverell, *Gondwana Theology: A Trawloolway man reflects on Christian Faith* (Melbourne: Morning Star, 2018), 71–72 for his reading of this passage.

be subject to critique from culture. This is the point, theologically, of listening to the voices of Indigenous culture. An example of culture's critique of gospel is the acute embarrassment now felt by churches at their earlier involvement in removing Indigenous children from their families.

There continues to be an ongoing debate, not least in Indigenous communities, about the compatibility between traditional culture and the gospel. Marion Maddox explored this debate in her study of the Hindmarsh Island bridge controversy in South Australia in the 1990s. She found that some Indigenous women opposed the claims of secret women's business at least partly because their own Christian faith had led them to reject elements of traditional culture, while others claimed the compatibility of traditional culture with Christian faith.[26] Part of the problem in any sharp distinction between Christianity and any particular culture, including an Australian Indigenous culture, is in fact theological. Christianity, because of its foundation in the incarnation, tends where to possible adapt itself to pre-existing cultural practices while also radically changing such cultural practices from within. This is a presupposition for my theological response below.

This raises the question as to what is meant by terms like 'religion', 'theology', and 'culture', and to what extent they are compatible or overlapping concepts. Here we have to resort to definitions, simply for clarity.

Geert Hofstede, one of the world's acknowledged authorities on cultures and inter-cultural communication, explains culture briefly in one place in this way:

> Culture has been defined in many ways; this author's shorthand definition is: '*Culture is the collective programming of the mind that distinguishes the members of one group or category*

---

26. Marion Maddox, 'How Late Night Theology Sparked a Royal Commission', in *Sophia: International Journal of Philosophical Theology and Cross Cultural Philosophy of Religion*, 36/2, 1997, 111–35; 'What is a "fabrication": The Political Status of Religious Belief', in *Australian Religion Studies Review*, 11/1 (1998): 5–16; 'Religious Belief in the Hindmarsh Island Controversy', in George Couvalis, *Cultural Heritage: Values and Rights*, edited by Helen Macdonald, and Cheryl Simpson (Adelaide: Proceedings of the 1996 International Conference on Cultural Heritage, Centre for Applied Philosophy, Flinders University, 3–4 October 1996), 61–79. Also at <https://mq.academia.edu/MarionMaddox> (accessed 5 July 2020).

of people from others.' It is always a collective phenomenon, but it can be connected to different collectives. Within each collective there is a variety of individuals. If characteristics of individuals are imagined as varying according to some bell curve, the variation between cultures is the shift of the bell curve when one moves from one society to the other. Most commonly the term culture is used for tribes or ethnic groups (in anthropology), for nations (in political science, sociology and management), and for organizations (in sociology and management).[27]

Hofstede is not totally consistent, resorting to other definitions in other places, but this just indicates the fuzziness of the concept. In any case, there is nothing here that would rule in or out an overlap with religion.

Definitions of religion are equally unclear. Peter Harrison demonstrates that it makes no sense to see a conflict between science and religion prior to the mid-19th century, simply because neither of these terms meant what they do now.[28] In the 16th century, for example, 'religion' meant something similar to what we now typically mean by 'spirituality'. Jared Diamond offers no less than sixteen definitions.[29] Stephen Prothero, in a book all about religions, simply refuses to define religion. What he does say, though, is that 'religion does not exist in the abstract. You cannot practice religion in general any more than you can speak language in general.'[30]

This in turn brings us to the nexus with language and culture in the attempt to understand religion, and here I refer to George Lindbeck's attempt at a definition, one that I have long found helpful in my own thinking:

---

27. Geert Hofstede, Hofstede, 'Dimensionalizing Cultures: The Hofstede Model in Context. Online Readings in Psychology and Culture, Unit 2.' (2011). See <http://scholarworks.gvsu.edu/orpc/vol2/iss1/8> (accessed 17 August 2020).

28. Peter Harrison, *The Territories of Science and Religion* (Chicago and London: University of Chicago Press, 2015).

29. Jared Diamond, *The World until Yesterday: What can we Learn from Traditional Societies?* (London: Penguin, 2013), 327–28.

30. Stephen Prothero, *God is not One: The Eight Rival Religions that Run the World & Why their Differences Matter* (Melbourne: Black Inc, 2010), 9.

> A religion can be viewed as a kind of cultural and/or linguistic framework or medium that shapes the entirety of life and thought. It functions somewhat like a Kantian *a priori*, although in this case the *a priori* is a set of acquired skills that could be different. It is not primarily an array of beliefs about the true and the good (although it may involve these), or a symbolism expressive of basic attitudes, feelings or sentiments (although these will be generated). Rather, it is similar to an idiom that makes possible the description of realities, the formulation of beliefs, and the experiencing of inner attitudes, feelings and sentiments. Like a culture or language, it is a communal phenomenon that shapes the subjectivities of individuals rather than being primarily a manifestation of these subjectivities.[31]

Religion, on these terms, is like a language (it is similar to 'an idiom') that helps people formulate and express their feelings and thoughts. It is a framework in which or a window through which we look at the world. It is a worldview. It is, in other words, very like a culture. It is also a set of skills that has to be learnt. Lindbeck's definition of religion likens it then to a cultural framework through which we view the world and try to make sense of it, or a language through which we try to articulate the meaning of what we experience, both as individuals and as communities.[32] We don't speak language in general (in the same way as there is no culture in general[33]); we speak a particular language (or if we're fortunate, particular languages—but even then we'll tend to favour one over others). In the same way we become (or fail to become) expert in making sense of experience by means of a certain matrix of references, and at the deepest level those are religious references. Meaning is brought to expression though a grammar, and we may become more expert in using this grammar.

A theology is the meta-level of thinking about how these skills are to be practised. For now suffice it to say that the territories of religion and culture are overlapping circles, with a great deal in common.

---

31. George Lindbeck, *The Nature of Doctrine: Religion and Theology in a Post-Liberal Age* (London: SPCK, 1984), 33.

32. This is the opposite of 'we had the experience but missed the meaning', TS Eliot, 'The Dry Salvages', in *Collected Poems 1909–1962* (London: Faber and Faber, 1963), 208.

33. Tanner, *Theories of Culture*, 66.

With regard to the meaning to theology, I accept Chris Budden's description: 'essentially a set of marginal notes that help people perform the Christian life.'[34] This is no different in intent from a more abstract definition offered by Dietrich Ritschl:

> Reflection by way of testing the function of regulative statements with reference to the thought and action of believers then and now. It tests statements for their comprehensibility, coherence and flexibility and aims at binding statements (truth). In this sense theology is not reserved for professional academics.[35]

In both cases theology is defined with 'reference to the thought and action of believers,' and 'is not reserved for professional academics'. Theological reflection, for Christians, is thinking within the framework of the Christian tradition as an aid to living authentically within that tradition. It aims at truth, and that means living truly and authentically—a matter to which we will return. I shall, admittedly, at times extend the scope of this term 'theology', as Gammage does when he talks of Indigenous theological knowledge, and when I consider what I shall call 'secular theology'. I take as axiomatic the insight of the radical orthodox school of thought that 'modern secular thought seeks to articulate something with only semi-coherence, since it fails to see that a fully coherent articulation requires the theological'.[36] This is a particular problem in Australia, for historical reasons to be outlined below, and this in turn makes it difficult for mainstream Second People Australian culture to hear from knowledge systems based not in analysis but participation.

Any dialogue between culture and theology is going to be a public exercise, simply because culture itself is never private, but held in common, in community. But religion, and with it, theology, has been relegated to a largely private space in common modern secular

---

34. Chris Budden, *Following Jesus in Invaded Space: Doing Theology on Aboriginal Land*, Princeton Monograph Series 116 (Eugene, USA: Pickwick, 2009), 82.
35. Dietrich Ritschl, *The Logic of Theology: A Brief Account of the Relationship Between Basic Concepts in Theology*, translated by John Bowden (Philadelphia: Fortress, 1987), xxii.
36. John Milbank, Graham Ward, Catherine Pickstock, 'Introduction: Suspending the Material: The Turn of Radical Orthodoxy', in *Radical Orthodoxy: A New Theology* (Routledge: London/New York, 1999), 6.

understanding. To what extent, we have to ask then, can theological reflection be a 'public' activity, with implications for public debate? Duncan Forrester argues that theology has, or should have, a public role:

> Public theology, as I understand it, . . . is theology which seeks the welfare of the city before protecting the interests of the Church . . . .. (It) seeks to offer distinctive and constructive insights from the treasury of faith to help in the building of a decent society, the restraint of evil, the curbing of violence, nation-building, and reconciliation in the public arena . . . It strives to offer something that is distinctive, and that is gospel, rather than simply adding the voice of theology to what everyone is saying already. Thus it seeks to deploy theology in public debate, rather than a vague and optimistic idealism which tends to disintegrate in the face of radical evil.[37]

Höhne and Oorschot reflect this idea in the criteria they use in their selection of public theology texts: a public theology must respect the rights of the margins, and the marginalised.[38] Public theology reveals a consistent preference for the prophetic and emancipatory strands in Christian theology. Public theology is not against nation-building, but it is selective in its interests: it is necessarily always contextual, and it must have different priorities from those of the world at large.[39] Rufus Black takes this idea of the public further by defining its conventional opposite, the 'private', in contrast not to the 'public' but to the personal, so that the personal can and must speak publicly:

> The private is the sanctuary of intimacy—of dreams, imaginings and prayers; it is a place to which we can issue invitations but to which nobody can demand access . . . So while prayer may be a private matter, beliefs in God and right and wrong are not . . . Much of religion belongs to the realm of

---

37. Duncan Forrester, 'The Scope of Public Theology', in *Studies in Christian Ethics*, 17 (2004): 6.

38. *Grundtexte Öffentliche Theologie*, edited by Florian Höhne and Frederike van Oorschot (Leipzig: Evangelische Verlagsanstalt, 2015), 9.

39. About the public nature of theology, see my 'Public Theology: A New Paradigm in Ecumenical Relations?', in *Ökumene ist keine Häresie. Theologische Beiträge zu einer ökumenischen Kultur*, edited by Daniel Munteanu (Leiden: EJ Brill, 2020 forthcoming).

> the personal rather than the private and, as such, should have
> its life in public spaces.[40]

The 'we' in the title of this essay is intended to refer both to the Australian public in general, as well as the Christian churches and their members. Theological reflections, here, may be personal, but are not intended to be merely private.

There is another reason for wanting to address this theologically. The dominant civilisation in Australia rests on a certain well-hidden but nevertheless real theological foundation. This theology, whose sacred text is the (rather selectively read) Bible and which has, in my opinion, many positives and some negatives, undergirds a certain set of attitudes to land, earth, and country. The Bible begins with a picture of dry earth emerging and ends with a vision of a new heaven and a new earth. It contains stories of conquests of lands, the promise of land, and for Christians, the central normative prayer, the Lord's Prayer, centres around the word 'earth'.[41] These are the texts and the stories that undergird, albeit rather anonymously, European civilisation in Australia. These texts and stories, furthermore, come to us through a particular modern European lens.

It is the anonymity and the interpretation of this theological foundation we need to take into account. The European settlement of Australia, unlike earlier European settlements outside of Europe, was not predominantly a religious settlement. The European civilisation that arrived so precipitately in 1788 was the civilisation of the European Enlightenment, with all the non-religious and even anti-religious aspects of that period. Its driving force was not faith, but commerce; its ideology was not religion but empire. Raewynne Whiteley has put it well: 'When the Australian colony was founded in 1788, it was celebrated with the raising of the British flag and copious amounts of alcohol, rather than with prayer or religious symbolism.'[42] Even though God's name is always held in reserve, to

---

40. Rufus Black, 'Theology and the Private, the Personal and the Public', in *Interface*, 3/1 (2000): 107–13, here at 107.

41. Vicky Balabanski, 'An Earth Reading of the Lord's Prayer: Matthew 6:9–13', in *Readings from the Perspective of Earth*, edited by Norman C Habel (Sheffield: Sheffield Academic press, 2000), 151–61.

42. Raewynne Whiteley, 'Church in Public Space', in '*Wonderful and Confessedly Strange': Australian Essays in Anglican Ecclesiology*, edited by Bruce Kaye, Sarah Macneil, and Heather Thomson (Adelaide: ATF Press, 2006), 379–405, here 384.

be brought out explicitly at significant moments to endorse loyalty
to the nation, religion in Australia has never held the place it did and
still does in the Americas or Southern Africa. A critique of colonial
culture in Australia will consequently be to some degree a critique of
secularism. It is essentially a secularist theology, or perhaps better,
secularist ideology, that underpins Australian national identity,
and that resists questioning from within its own framework. 'The
country, after all, was an experiment of the survival of the fittest, of
the unravelling,' says Tara June Winch. 'Darwin was even the name of
a town in the north.'[43] Grenville's Mrs Macarthur writes of the death
of the Indigenous resistance leader Pemulwuy: 'A settler shot him,
and to prove the fact cut off his head, which was sent to England
for the scientific gentlemen.'[44] This secularism may account for the
sometimes jarring lack of subtlety in references to church or religion
in Australian literature, as if Christianity were simply a matter of
some monolithic post-denominational institution.[45]

By secularism I do not intend any criticism of the secular
constitutions of societies that refrain from legitimising any particular
religious institution in preference to others. This notion of the secular
is simply a function of the freedom of religious allegiance, expression
and practice. By secularism I mean rather the opposite of the claim
of radical orthodoxy affirmed above: secularism is the ideology that
claims, as a matter of principle, that 'a fully coherent articulation' of the
world can be attained without recourse to theological insights. This
is the 'mainstream master narrative,'[46] whose hegemony, according
to Charles Taylor, is increasingly challenged by our contemporaries,
and properly so, because our 'sense of things, our cosmic imaginary'[47]
is left without their proper 'weight, gravity, thickness, substance . . .
There is a deeper resonance which they lack, which we feel should

---

43. Tara June Winch, *The Yield* (Melbourne: Hamish Hamilton, 2019), 84.
44. Kate Grenville, *A Room Made of Leaves* (Melbourne: Text, 2020), 312.
45. This religious illiteracy is not a new phenomenon: Henry Lawson pushed
    poetic licence to its limits in seeing difference in 'creed' between his presumably
    Anglican squatter and Presbyterian selector in his 1900 classic 'The Fire at Ross's
    Farm': <https://www.poetrylibrary.edu.au/poets/lawson-henry/poems/the-fire-
    at-rosss-farm-0002036> (accessed 27 July 2020).
46. Charles Taylor, *A Secular Age* (Cambridge, USA: Belknap, 2007), 534–35.
47. Taylor, *A Secular Age*, 325.

be there, according to Taylor.[48] This ideological secularism, which in its Australian manifestation is by no means uniform or monolithic,[49] is reductionist in attempting to confine theology, and more broadly, religious expression, to the sphere of personal taste and private opinion, and thus deny theology its proper public voice—within secular society.

Western civilisation has a certain bureaucratic culture and set of procedures for doing things: meetings procedure, rules for debate and voting, management styles, and accreditations of those whose word carries the greater authority. Indigenous Australia has a different set of 'protocols,' as Yunkaporta calls them. These two cultures encountered one another in 1788, with the result that the western cultural grid has been placed over the Indigenous culture. Australian governments still expect Aboriginal people and organisations to comply with this cultural grid. This expectation is something we need to question. Churches have also complied. This is, after all, our default way of looking at things and making decisions: it has been for a very long time, as is evident from the way ecclesiastical and civic governances have grown together and influenced each other. Church synods have shaped how parliament operates, and parliaments have in turn shaped synodical governance in the churches. The gospel points to a radically different way of governance, or better, of relating to one another. Jesus spoke with a different sort of authority from the conventional. For Christians, this should hold the potential to open up a conversation about new ways of doing things.

Non-Indigenous approaches to Indigenous cultures

The Australia ecologist Val Plumwood once spoke of a personal project of hers to decolonise the Australian landscape, by which she meant discarding, as relics of the colonial era, the many borrowed British placenames scattered over the map, and, where they are

---

48. Taylor, *A Secular Age*, 307.
49. On the variety of Australian secularisms, see Manning Clark, 'Faith', in *Occasional Writings and Speeches* (Melbourne: Fontana, 1980), 152–59; and John Docker, *Australian Cultural Elites: Intellectual Traditions in Sydney and Melbourne* (Sydney: Angus and Robertson, 1974).

known, restoring to use the Indigenous names of places.[50] The recent act of vandalism by the Rio Tinto mining company at a 46,000 year-old heritage site at Juukan Gorge, especially provocative because perpetrated just before the start of National Reconciliation Week in 2020, and the even more recent destruction of culturally significant trees near Ararat in Victoria, demonstrate just how far we still have to go in this regard.[51] Places are important in Australian Indigenous worldviews, and names are important in the biblical view of the world. So an acknowledgement of the original naming of places, as is slowly happening in some significant locations, may be an important theological statement as well as a symbolic step towards decolonisation. But it should not be merely symbolic; more importantly, it needs to be a step closer towards deeper listening to Indigenous voices.

In 1990, as part of the preparation for the seventh World Council of Churches Assembly, in Canberra, Muriel Porter named the treatment of Indigenous people at the top of her list of issues confronting spirituality in Australia.[52] Bill Gammage speaks to his fellow non-Indigenous Australians in warning that: 'We have a continent to learn. If we are to survive, let alone feel at home, we must begin to understand our country. If we succeed, one day we might learn to be Australian.'[53] This is part of what Celeste Liddle identifies as the nation's own need to 'grow up Aboriginal.'[54] Mark McKenna, whose Quarterly Essay has a whole section on 'listening to Indigenous voices,' calls on us to listen 'to Indigenous Australians as they tell us their histories in the spirit of Makarrata—healing and coming together after struggle'. In the light of Australian deep history, this

---

50. Val Plumwood, speaking at the National Ecotheology conference held in the Adelaide College of Divinity Campus, Adelaide, 1996.

51. Calla Wahlquist <https://www.theguardian.com/australia-news/2020/may/30/juukan-gorge-rio-tinto-blasting-of-aboriginal-site-prompts-calls-to-change-antiquated-laws> (accessed 30 May 2020); Timna Jacks, '"Not Listening": Sacred trees cut down for highway,' in *The Age*, 7 October 2020, 6; Miki Perkins, 'Anger of Felling of Historic Tree', in *The Age*, 27 October 2020, 7; Lidia Thorpe, 'I'm Heartbroken by this Colonial Violence', in *The Age*, 29 October 2020, 29.

52. Muriel Porter, *Land of the Spirit? The Australian Religious Experience* (Geneva: WCC/Melbourne: JBCE, 1990), 88–93.

53. Bill Gammage, *The Biggest Estate on Earth: How Aborigines Made Australia* (Sydney: Allen & Unwin, 2011), 323.

54. Celeste Liddle, 'Black Bum', in Heiss, *Growing up Aboriginal in Australia*, 153.

is the least we can do.[55] It is worth noting that these and other non-Indigenous writers like Sarah Maddison are explicitly responding to Indigenous voices.

Ros Moriarty's semi-autobiographical narrative is an account of her own acceptance into her husband's Aboriginal family, from which he had been separated in infancy but whom he rediscovered and with whom he had reconnected. At its heart is the story of her participation in a week-long women's ceremony. The ceremony itself is not, and may not be described to outsiders, but the attitudes and emotions surrounding it and her own acceptance into it, are described with a depth of respect and gratitude. These are summarised in her chapter titles and reveal a sense of cosmic and social purpose and belonging. The centrality of family connection and connection to country runs through the story from start to finish.

A specifically theological exploration of Indigenous culture is Eugene Stockton's study of Australian Indigenous spirituality.[56] Stockton sees the Aboriginal presence as holding out a gift to a multicultural Australian population, a 'taproot' deep into the rocky earth of this island continent:

> We are a collection of fragments of peoples gathered from around the globe. We form, as I have said, a single tree with roots reaching into every part of the earth, including a taproot which goes deep down into the soil of Australia. We rightly take pride in our respective roots, each keeping alive the memory of our ethnic past. But we are drawn together and shaped by a new-old land and by a recognition of shared human experience. If any good is to come of this nation, if any deep joy and hope is to arise from this union of many peoples, it will come from the perceived solidarity of all who have suffered. This is a key element in the developing religious outlook of Australia, what Les Murray has called 'the ritual of the Common Dish.[57]

---

55. McKenna, 75. 'Deep history' is a term used by a number of contemporary writers to refer to extraordinarily long antiquity and unbroken continuity of Indigenous culture in this country.
56. Eugene Stockton, *The Aboriginal Gift: Spirituality for a Nation* (Sydney: Millennium Books, 1995).
57. Stockton, *The Aboriginal Gift*, 21.

Stockton is critical of the shallowness of Second People religion in Australia and advises this needs to be deepened by mindful exercise of 'walking in and through country'.[58]

One of the perennial themes in these writings is that of place, its centrality in Australian Indigenous worldviews, and the corresponding sense of dis-placement in the overwhelming encounter with non-Indigenous society. An early cultural study of Australian worldviews that addresses this theme directly is that of Tony Swain.[59] Swain is concerned with ontology, the nature of being, in Australian Indigenous worldviews. These, he argues (in a critique of Eliade), involve neither linear nor cyclical notions of time, because time itself is not the basis of Australian ontology. Instead, place—defined by 'Abiding Events'—is the basis: Aboriginal people, prior to the intensive disruption by outsiders, had not allowed 'time' to develop as a determinative quality of being.[60]

Instead of time, space—not the 'homogeneous, abstracted' space of European thought from Euclid to the Deists—but space in the form of specific, concrete *places* is definitive of being: 'The basic and only unit of Aboriginal cosmic structure is the place.'[61] Place, or rather 'a plurality of places', for place is defined by personal relationships with the people who belong to that place, is the 'nucleus of Aboriginal ontology':[62]

> At every turn . . . Aboriginal people denied the possibility of self-sufficiency of being. There was an absolute, irreplaceable and fundamental identity between a land and a people who were spiritually of that land . . . Place, in its radical form—

---

58. Stockton, *The Aboriginal Gift*, 130.
59. Tony Swain, *A Place for Strangers: Towards a History of Australian Aboriginal Being* (Cambridge: Cambridge University Press, 1993). I use 'early' here because this survey limits itself essentially to writings in the past three decades.
60. Swain, *A Place for Strangers*, 20.
61. Swain, *A Place for Strangers*, 29. See Kate Rigby, *Topologies of the Sacred: The Poetics of Place in European Romanticism* (Charlottesville and London: University of Virginia Press, 2004) for a consideration of the transformation of concrete places into abstract space during the industrial revolution in Britain, a series of events and changes in perception that prepared the way for the abstraction of space in Australia.
62. Swain, *A Place for Strangers*, 44.

[is] unique and thus not self-sustaining but requiring relationship.[63]

While some of Swain's argument may have to be revised in the light of more recent scholarship,[64] it remains an important philosophical contribution to understanding Australian concepts of time and place. By focussing on ontology, Swain's concern is with what we might call worldview, that is notions of reality, rather than what he considers 'more superficial categories of "religion" or "mythology,"'[65] which I take to mean the phenomena of cultic practice or storytelling. Storytelling can be far from superficial, but Swain's concern to go deeper than the descriptive writings of earlier anthropologists is commendable. Certain practices can only be explained, according to Swain, in relation to this ontology: 'the newborn child is immediately placed in a small earthy depression from which it is then "born"— an act surely stating unambiguously that the child comes . . . from a location.'[66] Death becomes a 'return of place-being to place.'[67] This is a place of 'Abiding Events' of which the human life that has emerged is an expression or an 'outgrowth of a location,' and 'it is enough that the spirit has been restored to its place.'

Swain examines the consequences of Aboriginal contact with three groups of strangers: Melanesians of the Torres Strait, Europeans, and Macassans from the Indonesian archipelago, especially Sulawesi. Each of these groups had to be assessed by Australian Aboriginal people as to where they fitted in the traditional ontology of place. Among the conclusions Swain draws are that the most destructive result of these contacts has been the loss of connection to land, or more specifically, the places that used to define a person's sense of themselves, their own being in the world.

Swain's appraisal of the significance of place is supported by numerous authors, not all of whom refer specifically to Swain himself. Take for example Billy Griffiths' description of the visit to Canberra by Frank Gurrmanamana from Arnhem Land, as reported by Rhys

---

63. Swain, *A Place for Strangers*, 52–53.
64. Notably his claim on page 75 that Northern Australia intentionally refrained from become agricultural, in the light of Bruce Pascoe's thesis in *Dark Emu*.
65. Swain, *A Place for Strangers*, 280.
66. Swain, *A Place for Strangers*, 44.
67. Swain, *A Place for Strangers*, 45.

Jones: 'Here the land was empty of religious affiliation . . . Here was a vast *tabula rasa*, cauterised of meaning . . .'[68] For Gurrmanamana, land, to hold meaning, has to be a specific territory, country that is known intimately. Other land might be (or might have been) of significance for other Aboriginal Australians, but that significance was not arbitrarily transferable.

Bill Gammage is largely concerned with the cultural unity of the Australian continent, including Tasmania. This was, as the title of his book suggests, about land management, but underlying it was a common religious theme. All religion, according to Gammage, attempts to explain existence and regulate behaviour, and 'Aboriginal religion integrated these by assuming spiritual parity of all life.'[69] He cites Strehlow's definition of the Dreaming (the more common designation of what Swain has called 'Abiding Events') as 'The great and specifically Australian contribution to religious thought,' which allowed of no division between time and eternity, and which demanded adherence to two rules: obey the Law (or maybe better, the Lore[70]), and leave the world as you found it. And indeed, according to Gammage:

> Australia obeyed the Dreaming. By world standards this is a vast area for a single belief system to hold sway, and in itself cause for thinking Australia a single estate, albeit with many managers.[71]

These many managers, despite significant differences of culture and language, held a common understanding of how each person related to land and the Dreaming. This unity also explains the phenomena, described by Bruce Elder, of particular stories being passed around the continent in the form of ceremonial corroborees.

---

68. Billy Griffiths, *Deep Time Dreaming: Uncovering Ancient Australia* (Melbourne: Black Inc, 2018), 171. Griffiths gives a helpful definition of the 'Dreaming' (the more conventional term for what Swain calls Abiding Events): 'a self-referencing and self-affirming system of meaning' (292).
69. Gammage, *The Biggest Estate on Earth*, 123–24.
70. Glenn Loughrey argues for lore (with law as a subcategory of this). See Loughrey, *On Being*, 87–90. Stan Grant (*Talking to My Country* [Sydney: HarperCollins, 2017], 71) conflates these two concepts, 'lore and law'.
71. Gammage, *The Biggest Estate on Earth*, 124–25.

Being born on or near a song-line decides a person's most important totem, and being taught part of a song or dance legitimates being on the country it describes.[72] Totem is not just a badge, but 'a life-force stemming from and part of a creator ancestor': it transcends and unites people across kinship groups. These songs were taught from childhood, with 'the more you learn the more you are told. The most senior learning is always theological, and only the able and committed progress to its more complex realms.'[73] The art of song, dance, memory and ritual were 'voluminous and intricate:'[74]

> Local supremacy allied with wide geographical knowledge, continental connections, and a universal theology . . . made the entire continent structured and committed to making resources abundant, convenient and predictable.[75]

Plants and animals have souls, according to Gammage's reading of Indigenous thinking, and animal and plant sanctuaries were safeguarded around important Dreaming sites, so that these functioned as temporary sites of regeneration.[76] Animals could be culled to manage excess, but were also herded, not by compulsion but by making plentiful for them the food they preferred.[77] People stored food, but had no need to defend these stores, which were respected entirely on the basis of trust.[78] There was an initial welcome to strangers, because 'they were also of the Dreaming' and so needed to be accommodated.[79] 'In the white world savages had no place, though their souls might; in the Dreaming all things had a place, so new comers must be accommodated.'[80] These are very large claims, and minimise both the importance of obligatory relationships between particular groups, and the hostility that prevailed between some other groups.

---

72. Gammage, *The Biggest Estate on Earth*, 126.
73. Gammage, *The Biggest Estate on Earth*, 133.
74. Gammage, *The Biggest Estate on Earth*, 138.
75. Gammage, *The Biggest Estate on Earth*, 146. Gammage's reference to theology here is reason in itself for a theological response to be called for.
76. Gammage, *The Biggest Estate on Earth*, 281–85.
77. Gammage, *The Biggest Estate on Earth*, 211.
78. Gammage, *The Biggest Estate on Earth*, 299–300.
79. Gammage, *The Biggest Estate on Earth*, 308.
80. Gammage, *The Biggest Estate on Earth*, 311.

In 2009 Chris Budden, who describes himself as a non-Indigenous Australian and who writes theology from a Reformed perspective, published a book on the problem of doing theology in 'invaded space'. He begins uncompromisingly with a critique of the language of 'settlement' in Australian history: 'this is not a settled place but invaded space,' and 'second people are people who live on another's land, not as guests but invaders'.[81] This is not simply a functional thing; it is about how land is perceived. The title of Budden's book mirrors the notion of the conversion of concrete places to abstract space: 'In the European narrative, earth is turned into "landscape" (something seen from the outside and from a distance, as separate from us) and "real estate"'.[82] He presupposes, correctly, that 'the churches in Australia have internalized the values of an invading society and its racist and class-based explanations and justifications of invasion. This has made us, even with the best of intentions, unable to hear and see or speak words that provide justice'.[83] In summarising the context, in terms of the injustices perpetrated against Indigenous people over more than two centuries, Budden writes that the role of the churches collectively was that of 'a moral policeman rather than teller of meaning and, far too often, a servant of government policy'.[84] He sees in contemporary Australia a culture of avoidance of this past and present reality,[85] and in the face of new Indigenous voices, a crisis in this contemporary Australian culture. To this situation, theology must resume its true task of 'the art of naming where God is':

> Theology is essentially a set of marginal notes that help people perform the Christian life . . . My claim is that in Australia, we will neither read the text rightly nor enact the play properly without we have sat with Indigenous people and allowed them to shape our enactment and be part of the play.[86]

---

81. Chris Budden, *Following Jesus in Invaded Space: Doing Theology on Aboriginal Land*, Princeton Monograph Series 116 (Eugene, USA: Pickwick, 2009), 4–5.
82. Budden, *Following Jesus*, 72.
83. Budden, *Following Jesus*, 7.
84. Budden, *Following Jesus*, 31.
85. Budden, *Following Jesus*, 60–3 on the forms taken by this avoidance.
86. Budden, *Following Jesus*, 82. Budden has previously (78–80) introduced the idea of Christian life as drama.

For this, theology in Australia 'needs to relearn the art of speaking with and to the wider world'.[87] This brings Budden's attention back to the theme of context, in this case the context of the theologian personally, which he locates in a complex of four sets of dynamics: the way we speak about and to God, the question of order and justice, the nature and task of being church in Australia, and the issues of covenant and treaty.

This final theme, treaty, came to the fore in the national consciousness in 2017, fifty years after Aboriginal people were recognised as citizens in Australia, with the Statement from the Heart agreed upon by Indigenous leaders meeting at Uluru.[88] Budden has responded to this with an extended theological reflection on this specific issue of why Indigenous sovereignty is theologically important.[89] It is important as a step towards healing of the national psyche, because, as things currently stand 'our national story and identity are untrue. What does a people do when it discovers its foundations are not moral?'[90] To this question Budden says 'owning history and recognising sovereignty is a first step towards healing,'[91] and it will be a healing for all Australians:

> There is a level of fear that this place that people are supposed to make home is in the middle of Asia/Oceania. There is a sense of vastness that is terrifying and inhospitable . . . I think this is in part because the colonial narrative is about economic space and a white possession, an extended real estate rather than a place of belonging. Sovereignty threatens to unravel that ownership and yet, paradoxically, promises to make this a place that can be home.

I can testify personally to this experience of having been socialised into both a sense of the vastness and inhospitality of the land and the proud claim to ownership. The junior primary school I attended had

---

87. Budden, *Following Jesus*, 72.

88. National Constitutional Convention 2017 <https://www.referendumcouncil. org.au/sites/default/files/2017-05/Uluru_Statement_From_The_Heart_0.PDF> (accessed 5 July 2020).

89. Chris Budden, *Why Indigenous Sovereignty should matter to Christians* (Adelaide: MediaCom Education, 2018).

90. Budden, *Why Indigenous Sovereignty*, 38.

91. Budden, *Why Indigenous Sovereignty*, 34.

an assembly hall with more than life-sized murals at each end—at one end we faced, as very young children, a mural in heroic proportions, depicting the raising of the union jack at Sydney Cove in 1788.[92] The mural that loomed over us from behind depicted the ill-fated Burke and Wills expedition, white men on horses and camels in a vast brown landscape—as if to say, you might have the union jack above you, kids, but just watch yourselves in this country, it's dangerous.

Sovereignty is always about power and is assumed to mean a single order of power that negates all others, but Budden wants to rephrase this as a dialectic of different sources of power. Sovereignty frames the discourse, but

> If we can reframe the issue as a conversation about the way different orders engage with each other and see the state as just one sort of political institution and order, we may make some progress on this issue.[93]

Budden proposes to do this by understanding 'rights'—which as a western liberal concept, may not even be the best term to use— as being 'related to and interwoven with responsibilities'. It is also important, Budden continues, that the claim for sovereignty does not mean that First Peoples are placed outside the nation-state. They are part of this state but are 'raising issues about how they participate in the state'.[94] Budden draws on the biblical story of Naboth's vineyard as a critique of power and its abuse,[95] and interprets the Genesis 3 creation story as a critique of human transgression against land.[96]

A number of these writings considered above make oblique reference to Indigenous theology, for example Bill Gammage.[97] Others, like Swain's study of Indigenous ontology, address specifically theological questions, and do so in highly sophisticated ways. Budden's books are explicitly theological and addressed to a church-based readership.

---

92. Caulfield North Central School, now Caulfield Junior College. The murals are by Sir William Dargie.
93. Budden, *Why Indigenous Sovereignty*, 40.
94. Budden, *Why Indigenous Sovereignty*, 44–5.
95. Budden, *Why Indigenous Sovereignty*, 54.
96. Budden, *Why Indigenous Sovereignty*, 95.
97. Gammage, *The Biggest Estate on Earth*, 133.

Shadowy presences and real absences

It has long been noted that a great many significant Australian novels contain side-way glances to a silent Aboriginal presence.[98] Veronica Brady noted that Australian novels often have an Aboriginal figure just out of the focus, on the edge of the main action—but watching.[99] 'There are,' as Yunkaporta puts it, 'ghosts all over this massacre-soaked continent . . .'[100] The Indigenous presence was systematically written out of Australian culture and the Australian landscape for two centuries, and yet it always hovered on the edges.[101] The uncanny shadowy presence but real absence is symbolised in Kate Grenville's novel *The Secret River* by the rock carving of a fish over which the emancipist squatter Thornhill has, after the massacre of local people, built his home:

> Under the house, covered by the weight of Mr Thornhill's villa, the fish still swam in the rock. It was dark under the floorboards: the fish would never feel the sun again. It would not fade, as the others out in the forest were fading, with no black hands to re-draw them. It would remain as bright as the day the boards had been nailed down, no longer alive, cut off from the trees and light that it had swum in.

> Sometimes, sitting in the parlour in the red velvet armchair, Thornhill thought of it underneath him, clear and sharp on the rock. He knew it was there, and his children might remember, but his children's children would walk about on the floorboards, and never know what was beneath their feet.[102]

---

98. Tim Winton's *Cloud Street* (Melbourne: McPhee Gribble, 1991); Alex Miller, *Journey to the Stone Country* (Sydney: Allen & Unwin, 2003); and Lucy Treloar, *Salt Creek* (Sydney: Picador, 2015); are examples. But see Pascoe, 'Rearranging the Dead Cat,' in *Salt: Selected Stories and Essays* (Melbourne: Black Inc, 2019), 89–100, for a scathing reappraisal of this phenomenon.
99. Veronica Brady, Adelaide College of Divinity Annual Lecture, 'Spirituality and the Christian Religions in an Australian Context,' Flinders University 1992.
100. Yunkaporta, *Sand Talk*, 104.
101. One of the clearest examples of this is the inscription on the 1881 John Batman memorial in Melbourne's Queen Victoria Market, and its reference to 'the site of Melbourne then unoccupied'. Small plaques correcting this inscription and apologising to Indigenous people were added in 1992 and again in 2004.
102. Kate Grenville, *The Secret River* (Melbourne: Text Publishing, 2005), 316.

When, in her more recent novel, Kate Grenville's Mrs Macarthur finds a digging stick, she asks herself

> was it possible that it had been left as a message to me—one that I had been too obtuse even to recognise as a message? *This is my place, and this object shows that it is my place . . .* It was a shadow at the edge of my life, the consciousness that I was on land that other people knew was theirs. On the days I walked without glimpsing any of the Burramattagal, I was glad to pretend that there was no shadow.[103]

Tara June Winch has the central figure in her recent novel reflect on a similar shadow while living in England:

> She had thought about how everywhere in that place Romans had written the local people out of their history. She was trying to figure out how people valued a thing, what made something revered while other things were overlooked. Who decided what was out with the old, what had to have a replacement?[104]

Winch's character is, of course, reflecting primarily on the erasure of her own Indigenous Australian history.

But Aboriginal figures have taken increasingly significant roles in many novels, an increasing number of them by Aboriginal authors.[105] Beside Patrick White's novel based on the imagined life of Leichhardt in New South Wales and Northern Territory and Adam Courtney's partly-fictionalised account of the stories of John Batman and William Buckley in the Port Phillip District,[106] we can place Kim Scott's novel based on the history of the Swan River colony in Western Australia. To these we can add Julie Janson's *Benevolence*,[107] set in the Hunter

---

103. Kate Grenville, *A Room made of Leaves* (Melbourne: Text, 2020), 262.

104. Tara June Winch, *Yield* (Melbourne: Hamish Hamilton, 2019), 247.

105. Alexis Wright, *Carpentaria* (Sydney: Giramondo, 2006); Kim Scott, *Taboo* (Sydney: Picador, 2017); Tony Birch, *The White Girl* (Brisbane: University of Queensland Press, 2019); Leah Purcell, *The Drover's Wife* (Sydney: Hamish Hamilton, 2019); Tara June Winch, *The Yield*.

106. Patrick White, *Voss* (Sydney: Knopf, 2012); Kim Scott, *That Deadman Dance* (Sydney: Picador, 2011); Adam Courtney, *The Ghost and the Bounty Hunter* (Sydney: ABC Books, 2020).

107. Grenville, *The Secret River*; Julie Janson, *Benevolence* (Broome: Magabala, 2020).

River region, the recent response from the other side of the frontier to Kate Grenville's *The Secret River*. These tend to be the stories of Indigenous people welcoming strangers and then negotiating, or being prevented from negotiating, their survival from positions of rapidly decreasing technological and numerical advantage. Survival is a theme in many of the more recent personal stories of people who were separated from their families. Frank Byrne, talking about being taken away, to a place where family connections were deliberately broken up writes: 'This was the start of survival for me . . . I was only six years old and had to survive the best way I could.'[108] The recent novels by Aboriginal authors document resistance in the face of ongoing social disadvantage in contemporary Australia. These are voices that Australia must learn to hear.

One of the elements that come out in much of this literature is just how porous the frontier between Indigenous and non-Indigenous culture in Australia was and continues to be. It comes out in the constant crossing of cultural boundaries by the character of Muraging/Mary in Julie Janson's novel *Benevolence*; it comes out in many of the stories in Anita Heiss's collection, stories of people who even nowadays are discovering their own indigeneity. Bruce Pascoe puts it this way: 'if you passed two hundred people in Sydney's Pitt Street or Melbourne's Bourke Street this morning, it is likely that six of them would have been Aboriginal.'[109] The frontier in Australia was never the impervious barrier suggested by the word 'frontier,' and this is reason for hope that there can be an exchange of insights in and on this country, including in theology.

Several recent books from a self-consciously Aboriginal perspective demand a rewriting of Australian self-understanding. These works by Indigenous writers about Aboriginal Australian worldviews are hard to classify according to sources or standard academic methodologies. They cross academic boundaries: hence my reliance on fiction, poetry and autobiography as well as cultural, historical and theological studies. Key elements of Aboriginal worldviews are to be found in recent novels by Indigenous authors. Here I want to mention just two novels, by Alexis Wright and Tara June Winch, one extended prose-

---

108. Frank Byrne (with Frances Coughlan and Gerard Waterford), *Living in Hope* (Alice Springs: Ptilotus, 2018), 12–13, 35.

109. Bruce Pascoe, 'Rearranging the Dead Cat,' in *Salt*, 89–100, here at 98.

poem, by Ambelin Kwaymullina, and the autobiographical reflections of Stan Grant. Among reflections on Indigenous culture from within that culture, recent books by Bruce Pascoe, Tyson Yunkaporta and Victor Steffensen are explicit calls for non-Indigenous Australians to listen and respond, not simply for the sake of Indigenous people, but for the sake of country, specifically in order to care for country, and for places within country. These writers are explicitly directing their messages to wider audiences (Australian, in Pascoe's and Steffensen's cases, and worldwide, in Yunkaporta's case) because they believe *we* need to hear them. Although they raise theological issues, their primary focus is on country, land, earth, hence my use of the term 'ge-ologies'[110] to describe their genre. Though these writers address theological questions to some extent, we will come later to several explicitly theological works from Indigenous writers: the collective known as the Rainbow Spirit Elders, then books by Anne Pattel-Gray, Garry Deverell and Glenn Loughrey.

---

110. I use this hyphenated term to speak about reflection country, as a parallel to theologies, below, and to distinguish it from the more common use of 'geology'. Glenn Loughrey uses the adjective 'geophysical' (*On Being Blackfella's Young Fella* [Melbourne: Coventry, 2020], 47), but there is no elegant way of making a noun from this.

Indigenous Voices

Poetry and Storytelling: Alexis Wright, Tara June Winch, Ambelin Kwaymullina, Stan Grant

With Alexis Wright's long rambling novel *Carpentaria*, we are thrown into the deep end of an enchanted universe, in the Aboriginal settlement of Pricklebush, to the west of the fictional Carpentaria town of Desperance. 'Desperance' is a middle English word, meaning pretty much what it sounds like, that fell out of usage after the mid-sixteenth century, to re-emerge in far northern Australia in Wright's 2007 novel. The people of Pricklebush live in constant communication, not always friendly, with the inhabitants of the Dreaming, and in tension with both the Eastsiders, the other Aboriginal clan, most of whom are relatives, and the non-Indigenous inhabitants of Desperance, collectively known as Uptown, who are powerful, dangerous and stupid: 'there was no good whitefella government governing for *blackpella* people anywhere.'[1] For Uptown, God is absent,[2] and the white inhabitants *'don't even remember their own religion'.*[3] The constant undercurrent of memory of the historic massacres[4] do nothing to overcome the low level enmity within the Indigenous communities: 'The two senior men of the opposite clans never spoke, or acknowledged the other existed. Their language had no word for compromise.'[5] The 'old spirit wars' continue interminably.[6] Fights

---

1. Alexis Wright, *Carpentaria* (Melbourne: Giramondo, 2007), 126.
2. Wright, *Carpentaria*, 20.
3. Wright, *Carpentaria*, 49.
4. Wright, *Carpentaria*, 11, 102, 435.
5. Wright, *Carpentaria*, 380.
6. Wright, 372.

between Aboriginal women become a circus for the amusement of Uptown.[7]

The story is filled with faint echoes of other writers.[8] Who uses the term 'widdershins'[9] unless they're quoting Judith Wright, or happen to be regional Scottish? The allusions, which connect the world of Wright's novel to a larger literary universe, are often subtly humorous: Angel Day, the regal wife of Norm Phantom, is 'full of grace',[10] a connection highlighted later when she finds a statue of the Virgin Mary in the town rubbish dump, repaints it in Aboriginal colours, and much later, leaves the statue in charge of her house.[11] Wright's use of metaphor at times puts an ironic distance between the author and her characters, but one that in no way minimises the force of her critique of life in small town Australia, or the damage done to country by international mining companies.

At the centre of the district is the mine, against which Norm's son Will leads a protest, and is eventually involved in its destruction. Will Phantom knows local lore: When Will sees kingfisher 'Its flight was a part of the larger ancestral map which he read fluently.'[12] 'Will knew how the tides worked simply by looking at the movement of a tree, or where the moon crossed the sky, the light of the day, or the appearance of the sea. He carried the tide in his body.'[13] And true to his name, he can vanish from sight—a skill he and his siblings had perfected as children whenever the local policeman came by.[14] When Will is shot at, his companions see him 'disappear into the ground like he was made out of thin air'.[15] Even when he hides from his two older brothers, who almost see him, 'It was a wonder they did not hear his thoughts'.[16] This is the opposite of reductionism—it is assumed that brothers should be able to hear one another's thoughts. Everything in this world is purposeful: the mine worker chasing Will trips on

---

7. Wright, 222.
8. There are nods to Shakespeare, George Herbert, Mark Twain, Ernest Hemmingway and Patrick White, and probably many others I didn't notice.
9. Wright, *Carpentaria*, 194.
10. Wright, *Carpentaria*, 38.
11. Wright, *Carpentaria*, 338.
12. Wright, *Carpentaria*, 394.
13. Wright, *Carpentaria*, 401.
14. Wright, *Carpentaria*, 197.
15. Wright, *Carpentaria*, 405.
16. Wright, *Carpentaria*, 177.

'a rock that had, up to that moment, lain on the ground, embedded in soil that was thousands of seasons old, untouched by humankind since the ancestor had placed it in this spot, as if it had planned to do this incredible thing'.[17] There is the constant presence of the weird and magical, the ramshackled Phantom home 'guarded by black angels'.[18]

In this story, people mysteriously walk in from the sea to become gifts of God, or less mysteriously fall from the sky.[19] Will converses with Elias (while carrying his dead body):[20] death has no dominion in this country. By contrast, the white inhabitants of the Desperance Uptown are both shallow and dangerous. Aboriginal kids are instructed by their elders to go to school to *search through every single line of all those whitefellas' history books . . .*'[21](Yunkaporta would be pleased), and the protocol in Pricklebush has become 'you can't go upsetting the whites'.[22] The spirit of Australia is 'raw with unkindness',[23] with—in a reference to the mine—'poison festering in the souls of the men who disturbed the earth'.[24] 'The land [is] full of spirits. . . '.[25] Father Danny, the Irish hippy priest, a former heavyweight boxer, who has trained many 'good fighting Catholics' among the Aboriginal communities he serves, is the only white person to recognise these spirits. The novelist's portrayal of him is vivid with sympathetic humour.[26] When the mine is finally blown up, the Aboriginal spectators

> were sitting up there on the side of the hill—like rock wallabies, looking down at what was left of the Gurfurritt mine . . . What a turnout. Gee whiz! We were in really serious stuff now. We were burning the white man's very important places and wasting all his money. We must have forgotten our heads. We were really stupid people to just plumb forget like—because the white man was a very important person who was very precious about money.[27]

---

17. Wright, *Carpentaria*, 405.
18. Wright, *Carpentaria*, 201.
19. Wright, *Carpentaria*, 390.
20. Wright, *Carpentaria*, 195.
21. Wright, *Carpentaria*, 57.
22. Wright, *Carpentaria*, 97.
23. Wright, *Carpentaria*, 123.
24. Wright, *Carpentaria*, 175–76.
25. Wright, *Carpentaria*, 192.
26. Wright, *Carpentaria*, 185–90.
27. Wright, *Carpentaria*, 407.

The Aboriginal characters are confident in their prior placement in this land. To the local policeman, Will's sisters say 'We lit the fire to burn rubbish, so what if the wind started blowing the wrong way, that is what the wind was doing around here for thousands of years before Desperance ever existed.'[28] Remembering the old stories about how to live 'like a proper human being, alongside spirits . . .' was called *decorum* by their father, Norm Phantom.[29] At sea in the storm, Norm prays—but gets stuck 'on the perplexing word *trespass* . . . The word was weightless, but had caused enough jealousies, fights, injuries, killings, the cost could never be weighed. It maintained untold wars over untold centuries—*trespass*.'[30]

Just as Wright does not shy away from enmity and violence within Indigenous communities, neither does she whitewash the huge injustices against those communities. No one ever asks their opinions.[31] The Yinbirras, fairy-like people, had disappeared because they 'did not want their histories contaminated with oppression under the white man's thumb.'[32] The war against the mine had no rules. 'Nothing was sacred. It was a war for money,'[33] and Norm fears 'he had joined a dying race.'[34] His youngest son, Kevin, is set upon by white-hooded hoons and dies of his injuries, and there are the three boys dead in prison.[35] This passage has a dreamlike quality, as if to ask: is this really happening? But yes, it is. There is a contamination of the lakes near the mine: 'How many evolutions would it take before the natural environment included mines in its inventory of fear?'[36] There is the terrible memory in another town of racist graffiti and pack rape—dismissed as '*only a bit of taunting*.'[37] And the memories of the massacres—one character speaks in the dead language to 'his passed-away relatives.'[38]

---

28. Wright, *Carpentaria*, 225.
29. Wright, *Carpentaria*, 246.
30. Wright, *Carpentaria*, 267.
31. Wright, *Carpentaria*, 60.
32. Wright, *Carpentaria*, 299–300.
33. Wright, *Carpentaria*, 378.
34. Wright, *Carpentaria*, 303.
35. Wright, *Carpentaria*, 344, 358.
36. Wright, *Carpentaria*, 395.
37. Wright, *Carpentaria*, 450.
38. Wright, *Carpentaria*, 435.

The Uptown people continue to be stupid, cutting down trees (to rid the town of bats) even as a storm is brewing that will destroy the town, and only realising when 'the Bureau of Meteorology had called and translated the message from the ancestral spirits'.[39] The spirits (including the 'industrious guardian angel of good sense')[40] have been warning all along, but unheard by the non-Indigenous populace. Despite this, Will realises, when he hears the Italian mine worker 'singing the country in a foreign language, making the land and sea sacred to himself', that he also had been stupid to have thought in the old way (that the Europeans were simply shallow).[41] This new song is not so innocent—it has the capacity to take possession of the land and sea.

Tara June Winch's novel *The Yield*, set in the fictional but significantly named town of Massacre Plains, or simply Massacre as the local people call it, is the story of a young woman, August Gondiwindi, who has fled from her Indigenous community, gone for ten years almost as far away as it's possible to go, to London, but returns for the funeral of her grandfather, Poppy Albert.[42] On her return she discovers her grandfather has been making a dictionary of her traditional Wiradjuri language, and this sets her off on a journey of re-discovery of her own culture:

> Songlines—*yarang gudhi-dhuray* Means having line and *birrang-dhuray-gudhi* means journey having song. These lines are our early map-making. They measure our places, our impossible distances and they are passed down through story songs and dances. The lines are there, but sometimes the *gudhi* is lost. The Gondiwindi lost the *gudhi*, only now it's coming back to us again.[43]

This is, in the first instance, about place, and a form of map-making that is not about ownership, but the measuring of distances for the purpose of travel and encounter—with neighbours, but even more

---

39. Wright, *Carpentaria*, 466.
40. Wright, *Carpentaria*, 273.
41. Wright, *Carpentaria*, 386.
42. A theme familiar from Melissa Lucashenko's *Too Much Lip* (Brisbane: University of Queensland Press, 2018).
43. Tara June Winch, *The Yield* (Melbourne: Hamish Hamilton, 2019), 103.

importantly, with the land itself. The fundamental, life-shaping attitude this requires is one of respect:

> Respect—*yindyamarra* I think I've come to realise that with some things, you cannot receive them unless you give them too. Only equals can share respect, otherwise it's a game of masters and slaves—someone always has the upper hand when they are demanding respect. But *yindyamarra* is another thing too, it's a way of life—a life of kindness, gentleness and respect at once. That seems a good thing to share, our *yindyamarra*.[44]

Respect for country means, as it does in Wright's novel, opposition to the mining company that is trying to take possession of Massacre Plains, and August finds herself drawn into this opposition. Indigenous life, however, is not all kindness, gentleness and respect, and August feels intense shame at learning what a relative of hers has done: 'He has drained from who we are like *guwang* (i.e. blood) leaving the body. In that case water is thicker than blood.'[45] This sense of shame, however, is part of something much larger: 'Other people didn't have lumps in their throat year in and out, century after century. They didn't know what it was like to be torn apart.'[46]

Winch's novel is not without its own elements of theological reflection, which is not quite the same thing as religion. One of August's early memories is of her grandfather emphatically demythologising the Bible:

> *This is a book* her poppy had said the first time he placed one in her hands, speaking with fortified sureness. *I want you to read it as if every sentence inside it is a lie and, if you find anything true, I want you to write it down.*[47]

It is the sort of exercise in religious education that Kierkegaard would have approved of, and August does in fact find something to write down. This is not the end of August's education by her grandfather: 'He told me that Biyaami is the creator, but we don't worship Him or His

---

44. Winch, *The Yield*, 106.
45. Winch, *The Yield*, 255.
46. Winch, *The Yield*, 267.
47. Winch, *The Yield*, 114 (author's italics).

son. We worship things He made, the earth.'[48] August's grandfather is a man in constant conversation with his ancestors, one of whom (his pre-invasion, pre-massacre great-great-great grandfather) tells him at the end of his life 'you are resurrected, a man brought back from extinction!' Albert Gondiwindi at that point feels 'like an initiated man'.[49]

The prose-poem by Ambelin Kwaymullina is a manifesto: 'You are living on stolen land/What can you do about it?'[50] It begins with a declaration of love for country: trees, rivers, hills and stars—for country that has been stolen:

> There is no part of this place
> that was not
> is not
> cared for
> loved
> by an Aboriginal or Torres Strait Islander nation.[51]

There is not just one Indigenous nation:

> There is not one Indigenous sovereignty
> there are many.[52]

Settlement is worse than invasion. Invasion might strip a country of its wealth, but the invader eventually goes away. The settler does not. Invasion is temporary; settlement is permanent:

> Those who are not Indigenous to this land
> are Settlers
> This does not mean
> being a part of peaceful settlement
> It means
> being part of settler-colonialism
> a form of colonisation
> where invaders came
> and never left.[53]

---

48. Winch, *The Yield*, 254.
49. Winch, *The Yield*, 256.
50. Ambelin Kwaymullina, *Living on Stolen Land* (Broome: Magabala, 2020), 6.
51. Kwaymullina, *Living on Stolen Land*, 3.
52. Kwaymullina, *Living on Stolen Land*, 7.
53. Kwaymullina, *Living on Stolen Land*, 3–4.

Invasion involves chaotic violence; settlement follows with the structured violence of removals, surveillance, and the systematic suppression of culture. It leaves no place of innocence:[54] it is fall and apocalypse all at once. The language itself carries biblical resonances: where are your Settler stories, Kwaymullina asks, that speak of respect, humility, and relationship?[55] Settlers fail to understand Indigenous people, in two ways: we have wrong information, and our way of understanding is wrong. Our methodology is wrong, so, even with the best of intentions, we are in constant danger of misconstruing, misinterpreting, misapplying, and perhaps worst, of misappropriating.[56] By contrast:

> In Indigenous systems
> knowing
> comes from understanding
> how we connect
> to all the life around us
> and how all the life around us
> connects to each other.[57]

There can be, beside structural and explicit forms of bias, also unconscious bias—this 'the most difficult to shift,' for 'it is best at hiding'.[58] Two ways of being wrong, three forms of bias, and four typical settler behaviours—only one of which is appropriate.[59] But there are pathways out of this predicament, according to Kwaymullina. These are humility (which is not a feeling), listening (which has to be done right),

> Listening
> can be an act
> of transformative power
> provided
> it is done right[60]

---

54. Kwyamullina, *Living on Stolen Land*, 6.
55. Kwyamullina, *Living on Stolen Land*, 11.
56. Kwyamullina, *Living on Stolen Land*, 33–34.
57. Kwaymullina, *Living on Stolen Land*, 26.
58. Kwaymullina, *Living on Stolen Land*, 40.
59. Kwyamullina, *Living on Stolen Land*, 42–47.
60. Kwaymullina, *Living on Stolen Land*, 54.

and asking how (not what). Listening, however, has to be both purposeful and respectfully reticent:

> Listening means
> giving time and space
> for Indigenous peoples to decide
> what we want to share
> on what terms we want to share it
> or if we want to share it at all.[61]

This is a strengths-based approach, a set of pathways that look not to deficit but to empowerment. It is violence that always reveals a deficit—of power, as Hannah Arendt has told us,[62] or in this case, a deficit of real authority. Kwaymullina speaks with authority.

Stan Grant is well-known in Australia as a journalist and a political and social commentator. His preferred self-designation, however, is story-teller: 'I am a storyteller. I try to connect people to our shared humanity.'[63] It is an identity he shares with his great-grandfather, and 'something,' he says, 'that makes sense of the life I have lived. It connects me to my love of words and stories.'[64] His writings about Aboriginality are largely autobiographical, but they take us to familiar themes: country, identity, and above all, the intense pain of a history that is still present—and present not only in the imagination. He begins with the pain of what he has to say: 'It is not easy, what I have to say, and it should not be easy. These are things that tear at who we are . . . Things that kill . . . that drive people to suicide, that put us in prisons and steal our sight.'[65] Speaking of his family, he writes: 'We came from a long line of people who had been battered. These people found themselves outside the grand sweep of this country's progress. We were black and Australia was white.'[66] Despite the battering and marginalisation, there is huge sense of the inherent dignity of particular family members. Speaking of his own

---

61. Kwaymullina, *Living on Stolen Land*, 57.

62. Hannah Arendt, *On Violence* (New York: Harcourt, Brace and World, 1969), 56.

63. Stan Grant, *Talking to My Country* (Sydney: HarperCollins, 2017), 186.

64. Grant, *Talking*, 86.

65. Grant, *Talking*, 1. Later in the book Grant gives us the horrifying figures: three per cent of the Australian population, but a quarter of the prison population; in juvenile detention half the inmates are Indigenous (105–6; 109).

66. Grant, *Talking*, 23.

Aboriginal contemporaries at the age of fifteen, 'These kids could have powered their communities. But the tyranny of low expectations smothered them.'[67] Grant goes on to describe how he experienced these low expectations, when, against official government policy, the local school principal attempted to persuade a group of them to leave and find work, in effect 'reminding us that if we did have a place in Australia it would be on the margins.'

Grant tells how he found his later work as a journalist in places of war and natural disaster

> . . . took me into the lives of people in pain and misery. I was drawn to their stories . . . it was the common humanity of those whose existence was determined by forces bigger than themselves. I wanted to know how they found the courage to face another day when all certainty had been stolen from their lives.[68]

Grant seeks in these people an answer to his own questions. And here is yet another theft that went along with the theft of lands and languages and cultures, and later of children: the theft of all certainty. 'It happens like this sometimes as a reporter,' he writes, 'something speaks to me, compels me to listen'[69]—to listen to these stories that mirror his own community's experience, in which 'the weight of history in Australia suffocates us.'[70] This in itself, for a non-Indigenous Australian reader, is a startling thing to hear. We think we have so little history, and what little we have is free of the heavy, suffocating histories of other lands: we are, as we tell ourselves, 'young and free'. Towards the end of the book Grant writes 'we just can't take any more pain,'[71] and about how it feels to be Indigenous, 'it feels hard—and we are tired.'[72] This, it seems to me, is reason enough to refrain from *any* action or development—mines, roads, or whatever—that might add to this burden, at least until we have sat for a time and really listened.

---

67. Grant, *Talking*, 44–45.
68. Grant, *Talking*, 134. At this point Grant tells the story of a Palestinian refugee who had carried a jar of dirt from his homeland; I found myself asking, did my ancestors bring a jar of soil from home? If they did, it's long lost.
69. Grant, *Talking*, 136.
70. Grant, *Talking*, 117.
71. Grant, *Talking*, 190.
72. Grant, *Talking*, 213–14.

When Grant speaks about his return to his own Wiradjuri country, he writes:

> I was raised here: this place is alive to me . . . The effect it has on me is physical. When I am home I breathe more deeply. I sleep long and still. I wake to the morning more slowly.[73]

> I can hear this land talking to me, and it is always subdued. There is a magical connection that shows itself in unexpected ways.[74]

And he tells the story of one of those unexpected moments. In this place, time becomes irrelevant

> In my family's telling, time was not important—what happened yesterday was as real today and would be again tomorrow. What happened to my forebears felt as real as if it had happened to me.[75]

It is here that

> Spirits are not strange to us. They are not relegated to the realm of fantasy. The believers and the seers are not mocked. We like being scared. But there's another reason: we live closely with death. Death stalks our people. It can take us young, sometimes before we have even had a chance at life. Death comes with a warning, animals transformed into prophets of doom.[76]

Stan Grant is Indigenous and a news reporter, but, he says, 'I made a conscious decision that I would not be the "indigenous reporter". I railed against this straightjacket. I had seen other black people embark on careers . . . only to be marginalised.'[77] Identity, he finds, is complex. 'My fight with history is a battle within myself.'[78]

---

73. Grant, *Talking*, 7.
74. Grant, *Talking*, 162–63.
75. Grant, *Talking*, 177.
76. Grant, *Talking*, 99.
77. Grant, *Talking*, 126.
78. Grant, *Talking*, 68.

Grant's objection is to any one-dimensional identity, a theme he develops in his more recent book:[79] 'Identity does not liberate; it binds.'[80] 'Identity becomes a prison-house. We are locked in with those who are deemed our own company. It is the prison house of our own imaginations—these fictions, these stories carefully woven from collective memories that are not even one's own . . . what happened to our ancestors becomes what happened to us.'[81] It is this very seductive self-enclosed identity that Grant rejects: 'Is say no to this. I say no to breathing someone else's life.'[82] It is a rejection of all identity-politics, because life is more complex and multi-layered than this. 'To write against identity is to choose life,' and to move beyond the 'thinness of the polemicist.'[83] 'We are not what others insist we are'[84] and for this reason Grant insists (with reference to Australian government forms requiring information about a person's indigeneity), 'I will not put a mark in a box that someone else has decided contains me.'[85] 'I choose another definition of who I am . . . It is so simple I can say it in plain English and in one sentence: I will not be anything that does not include my grandmother.'[86] Instead of a one-dimensional (in this case, indigenous) identity, Grant chooses the way of love—something he learnt from his indigenous family:[87] 'Let me tell you something else about love: totalitarians hate love; but they love identity.'[88] Stan Grant speaks here of love as the one thing that negates all conventional markers of identity.

Talking to My Country ends with accounts of several relatively recent events that have begun to reshape the Australia we live in. Some have been positive: the Mabo case and the Redfern speech in 1992, Cathy Freeman at the Sydney Olympics in 2000, the apology to the stolen generations in 2008. Some have been at best ambiguous: the intervention in 2007. Some seem like steps back into the ever-present

---

79. Grant, Stan, *On Identity* (Melbourne: Melbourne University Press, 2019).
80. Grant, *On Identity*, 43.
81. Grant, *On Identity*, 58–59.
82. Grant, *On Identity*, 62.
83. Grant, *On Identity*, 63, 71.
84. Grant, *On Identity*, 72.
85. Grant, *On Identity*, 83, *cf* 22.
86. Grant, *On Identity*, 83.
87. Grant, *On Identity*, 19.
88. Grant, *On Identity*, 73.

past: the Adam Goodes saga in 2015. 'Australia,' Grant says, 'still can't decide whether we were settled or invaded. We have no doubt. Our people died defending their land and they had no doubt.'[89] In the end, however, acceptance and generosity of spirit win over anger. Speaking of non-Indigenous farming people, he writes:

> I have met these people; many of them have a deep love of this country. They have begun to see it as we do. Wherever their ancestors may have begun their journeys it is here that these people have been formed.[90]

But the pain is not so easily overcome.

Ge-ologies: Bruce Pascoe, Tyson Yunkaporta, Victor Steffensen

Bruce Pascoe also calls himself a storyteller,[91] so that categorising Indigenous writers into genres once again shows itself to be arbitrary. Pascoe's *Dark Emu*[92] is a sustained argument that pre-European Australia was not simply a hunting and gathering society, but an agricultural society. The significant thing about this book is its reliance on diaries and reports by nineteenth-century European observers of country and customs to refute the common stereotypes of 'primitive' peoples and cultures. Pascoe acknowledges at one point in his later book *Salt* that 'if the country had to be colonised—and that was inevitable—you could do worse than the British'.[93] Pascoe insists that Aboriginal society as it was in 1788 met the preconditions for being considered 'civilised' under the British law of the colonisers, and that conventional Australian history has deliberately erased all reference to Indigenous agriculture and sedentary farming life. Bruce Pascoe's work is a call for truth-telling: truth about what he sees as the agricultural past of Indigenous communities in Australia,

89. Grant, *Talking*, 2.
90. Grant, *Talking*, 24.
91. Bruce Pascoe, 'Andrew Bolt's disappointment,' in *Griffith Review*, 36, https://www.griffithreview.com/editions/what-is-australia-for/(accessed 19 October 2020).
92. Bruce Pascoe, *Dark Emu: Aboriginal Australia and the Birth of Agriculture* (Broome: Magabala Books, 2018).
93. Bruce Pascoe, ''Dear John, in *Salt: Selected Stories and Essays* (Melbourne: Black Inc, 2019), 171–79, here at 171.

and truth about the acts of violence that have been and continue to be perpetrated against these communities. Both forms of truth-telling are necessary for any healing of the national psyche. What we need, he argues, is 'a true conversation about what has been lost and what gained, and how that has forged the schizophrenic national psychology'.[94] 'There is nothing postcolonial about Australia. It still has a Raj mentality and a vindictive adherence to colonial myth.'[95] My concern about Pascoe's argument in *Dark Emu* is that it might seem to endorse the old anthropological hierarchy that places agriculture above hunting and gathering.

Pascoe is particularly critical, in his collection *Salt*, of the Abrahamic God as nothing more than an invention for the purpose of dominating both nature and Indigenous peoples, because this has been the experience of many Indigenous people in Australia.[96] 'We know that the assumption of others' land was related directly to the Christian religion.'[97] Bruce Pascoe claims to speak from his own lived experience, and this experience has to be heard. The churches and the mediation of the gospel have been tied to the colonial reality: 'Gospel and mission of the church,' in Budden's words, 'was shaped and still is shaped by its relationship with colonial empire.'[98] But this is where I have to admit to a degree of dissatisfaction with Bruce Pascoe's position. Pascoe is a perceptive reader of Australian literature, but he has not been able to bring the same sensitivity to his reading of the biblical texts. He misses the polyphonous dimension of the stories of this Abrahamic God, the fact that there can be differing and even contradictory meanings and priorities embedded in these texts.

The fact that Bruce Pascoe's view of Christianity (and indeed the Abrahamic traditions generally) relies on one single set of stories, and one scriptural theme, that of the imperial god, unfortunately undermines the really important things he has to say. Pascoe is correct in saying (white) Australia likes to 'see itself in the best possible light—a nation of knockabout larrikin mates who don't take

---

94. Bruce Pascoe, 'Temper Democratic, Bias Australian,' in *Salt*, 57–72, here at 65.
95. Pascoe, 'Temper Democratic, Bias Australian,' in *Salt*, 57. Sarah Maddison's *Colonial Fantasy* is also an extended engagement with this reality.
96. Pascoe, 'The Imperial Mind,' in *Salt*, 27ff.
97. Pascoe, The Galapagos Duct,' in *Salt*, 299–307, here at 300.
98. Chris Budden, *Why Indigenous Sovereignty should matter to Christians* (Adelaide: MediaCom Education, 2018), 60.

themselves too seriously and are not prepared to chew the rag of regret'.[99] The only thing I would add to Pascoe's description is that we Australians like to see ourselves as *likeable* larrikins.[100] What Pascoe fails to notice is that regret is a deeply Christian sentiment inspiring the active virtue of repentance; that is, not stopping with the sentiment alone, but going on to make amends for that which is regretted. It is one of the elements Nietzsche saw as so distasteful in Christianity. Pascoe does acknowledge that 'the greatest attendance at Christian churches is by Aborigines'.[101] Pascoe is correct in recognising one source of the imperial mind, the fact that, as Budden puts it, 'empires require two things . . . that the gods support them, and that there is only one, unifying story'.[102] Pascoe does not take account, however, of Budden's other point, that in the Bible 'sovereignty is shaped by covenant,'[103] and that within this framework different sovereignties can coexist. Pascoe concludes his collection with the statement 'I'm an agnostic, but I'd quite happily settle for a country that operated exclusively according to the Ten Commandments'.[104] To this I find myself reminded of the story of Karl Barth's response to a similar sentiment by First Secretary Walter Ulbricht in the newly established East Germany in 1946: 'Yes . . . especially the first' (commandment).[105] When he ventures into the realms of the metaphysical Pascoe seems a long way from the magical universe of Alexis Wright's Carpentaria. He might consider Budden's argument that 'I still think that the loss of God better serves those with power than those without.'[106]

---

99. Pascoe, 'Rearranging the Dead Cat,' in *Salt*, 89–100, here at 92.
100. I would call this habit of thinking ourselves *likeable* the Rostov delusion, after Tolstoy's character Nikolai Rostov, who after falling off his horse is surprised to find people are shooting at him: 'They can't want to kill me! *Me*. Everybody loves me!' Leo Tolstoy, *War and Peace*, translated by Anthony Briggs (London: Penguin, 2005), 200.
101. Pascoe, 'Dear John,' in *Salt*, 171–79, here at 176.
102. Chris Budden, *Why Indigenous Sovereignty should matter to Christians* (Adelaide: MediaCom Education, 2018), 61.
103. Budden, *Why Indigenous Sovereignty*, 56.
104. Pascoe, 'An Enemy of the People,' in *Salt*, 189–98, here at 194.
105. Eberhard Busch, *Karl Barth: His life from letters and autobiographical texts*, translated by John Bowden (London: SCM, 1975), 340.
106. Budden, *Why Indigenous Sovereignty*, 88–89.

Tyson Yunkaporta writes 'to provoke thought' in a 'kind of dialogical and reflective process with the reader' that he calls 'yarning' and for which he uses a vivid dual pronoun to translate a Cape York expression: 'us two'.[107] To this process of yarning that requires reciprocity[108] and stimulates 'connective thinking' he adds 'sand-talk', images, usually drawn in the sand to convey traditional knowledge. Yunkaporta has such a direct and colourful turn of phrase that he frequently deserves quoting verbatim. His aim is not to take on the imposed colonial system in a confrontation from the outside, a tactic he regards as ineffective (because, like it or not, we are all *within* this system), but for 'us two' to influence it from within.[109] Yunkaporta sees himself not so much writing about Indigenous culture as writing about the current global systems from an Indigenous Knowledge perspective.[110] For this purpose an Indigenous person, as mentioned above, is defined in a very inclusive way as 'a member of a community retaining memories of life lived sustainably on a land-base, as part of that land-base'.[111]

Sustainability is a key concept in Yunkaporta's book: 'I don't think most people have the same definition of sustainability that I do. I hear them talking about sustainable exponential growth while ignoring the fact that most of the world's topsoil is now at the bottom of the sea'.[112] What he rejects most strongly is the danger of a new sort of assimilation in which Indigenous people are civilised into positions of power within the current global systems:

> I remain troubled by the potential risk of creating Indigenous civilisations, Anglo economic systems administered by men with black faces but still following the same unsustainable global blueprint of destruction.[113]

---

107. Tyson Yunkaporta, *Sand Talk: How Indigenous Thinking Can Save the World* (Melbourne: Text, 2019), 22–23. Old English had such a dual personal pronoun, but one that has (unfortunately) been lost: see Norman Davis (editor) *Sweet's Anglo-Saxon Primer*, 9th edition (Oxford: Oxford University Press, 1957), 22.
108. Yunkaporta, *Sand Talk*, 236: A conversation in which 'you can't get a word in edgeways' is not really a yarn.
109. Yunkaporta, *Sand Talk*, 49.
110. Yunkaporta, *Sand Talk*, 15.
111. Yunkaporta, *Sand Talk*, 41–42.
112. Yunkaporta, *Sand Talk*, 59.
113. Yunkporta, *Sand Talk*, 245.

Sustainability depends on ongoing dialogue, and response to dialogue:

> Adaptation is the most important protocol of an agent
> in a sustainable system. You must allow yourself to be
> transformed through your interactions with other agents
> and the knowledge that passes through you from them. This
> knowledge and energy will flow through the entire system in
> feedback loops and you must be prepared to change so that
> those feedback loops are not blocked.[114]

Human beings are custodial creatures; custodians, that is, caretakers, of country and places on country.[115] Again and again, Yunkaporta returns to the idea of complex systems in nature, in plant, animal and human communities. This is an ecological thinking that emerges from patient listening: You have to show patience and respect, come in from the side, sit awhile and wait to be invited in:[116]

> The patterns and innovations emerging from these ecosystems
> of practice are startling, transformative and cannot be designed
> or maintained by a single manager or external authority. They
> cannot even be imagined outside of a community operating
> this way. This is the perspective you need to be a custodian
> rather than an owner of lands, communities or knowledge.
> It demands the relinquishing of artificial power and control,
> immersion in the astounding patterns of creation that only
> emerge through the free movement of agents and elements
> within a system . . . Pre-industrial cultures have worked within
> self-organising systems for thousands of years . . .[117]

By contrast, 'Western knowledge systems are centralised, and this could be why they have so far been unable to engage in dialogue with Indigenous Knowledge systems in the development of sustainability solutions.'[118] This surprisingly generous assessment by Yunkaporta, that we westerners are ourselves trapped in non-dialogical systems of

---

114. Yunkaporta, *Sand Talk*, 99–100.
115. 'Custodianship,' a term that becomes significant in Norman Habel's ecological theology, can be problematic, as I discovered at a theological conference in the UK: the British audience associated 'custodianship' with imprisonment rather than caring responsibility.
116. Yunkaporta, *Sand Talk*, 29.
117. Yunkaporta, *Sand Talk*, 94.
118. Yunkaporta, *Sand Talk*, 96.

thinking and self-organising, articulates a central problem in policy-making in Australia from the earliest European settlement till today: what we have in Australia is an encounter between two completely different ways of looking at and understanding the world, in which one set of cultural assumptions has been superimposed over the other. Western civilisation has a certain bureaucratic way of doing things, and a set of axiomatic procedures. Much like Hoddle's rectangular grid plan for Melbourne, as Adam Courtney describes it,[119] superimposed over rolling hills and gullies, straight lines beside a meander in the river, this essentially transactional, utilitarian and universalist model of what is considered appropriate and right has been imposed onto far more ancient relational and localised patterns of governance and daily life. The latter have been expected to conform themselves to the former: 'We think something terrible must have happened in the north to make people forget, causing science to have to start all over again from scratch rather than building on what went before.'[120]

To this situation, Yunkaporta insists:

> Sustainability agents have a few simple operating guidelines, or network protocols, or rules if you like—connect, diversify, interact and adapt. Diversity is not about tolerating difference or treating others equally and without prejudice. The diversification principle compels you to maintain your individual difference, particularly from other agents who are similar to you . . . You must seek out and interact with a wide variety of agents who are completely dissimilar to you. Finally, you must interact with other systems beyond your own, keeping your system open and therefore sustainable.'[121]

This is not simply a matter of justice, or even common sense as a way of avoiding conflict: it is a matter of basic sustainability. And the truth of it cannot be conveyed simply in transactional or utilitarian language. It must resort, like all discourse that seeks to address matters of what Paul Tillich called 'ultimate concern', to metaphor. Here, for example, is Yunkaporta writing about the symbolic content of smoking ceremonies:

---

119. Adam Courtney, *The Ghost & the Bounty Hunter: William Buckley, John Batman and the theft of the Kulin Country* (Sydney: ABC Book 2020), 256.
120. Yunkaporta, *Sand Talk*, 38.
121. Yunkaporta, *Sand Talk*, 98–99.

> Here's how the smoke works. It is made by the leaves: light
> from the sky camp and nutrients from under the ground,
> connecting the two worlds and moving between them, visible
> but intangible. You have to feel it go right through you ... The
> smoke is liminal—neither earth nor air but parts of both—so
> it moves across the same spaces in-between as shadow spirits
> do, sending them on their way.[122]

> Even written words are metaphors that help carry
> communication between the abstract and the practical realms
> ... Metaphors are the language of spirit.[123]

Even though not utilitarian, this way of knowing retains its practicality,
its concrete relevance to living on this country. In fact it is supremely
well adapted to the land. Furthermore, it is not so foreign to the
consciousness of Second Peoples:

> Knowledge transmission must connect both abstract
> knowledge and concrete application through meaningful
> metaphors in order to be effective ... Working with metaphor
> is a point of common ground between Aboriginal and non-
> Aboriginal knowledge systems ...[124]

Acknowledgement of this role of metaphor is about maturity in
a culture; it is about remembering the wisdom that has been lost
or buried beneath the multifarious perceived needs of industrial
societies. This is not a matter of some romantic return to Eden, or
a luddite rejection of modern science and technology. Rather, it is
a plea for remembering the elders and their wisdom. It does not
idealise Aboriginal cultural knowing (except insofar as it possesses
deep insight into the practicalities of living in *this* country), but calls
for rediscovering the wisdom embedded in all Indigenous cultures:

> Inspirational connections to unseen inner and outer worlds
> are a part of Aboriginal Knowledge transmission all over this
> continent. This connection is interwoven with every learning
> experience within the communities of First Peoples. It is ritual.
> It is the force that animates all Aboriginal Knowledge—a

---

122. Yunkaporta, *Sand Talk*, 107.
123. Yunkaporta, *Sand Talk*, 110. Yunkaporta rejects the term 'Dreaming,' 22.
124. Yunkaporta, *Sand Talk*, 118.

spirit of genius that shows the difference between yarning and conversation, Story and narrative, ritual and routine, civility and connectedness, information and knowledge. Most of all, it highlights the massive divide between engagement and compliance . . .[125]

Again, this is not unique to Indigenous cultures—it is to be found in every human culture, if we look deep enough:

I have previously talked about civilised cultures losing collective memory and having to struggle for thousands of years to gain full maturity and knowledge again, unless they have assistance . . . The assistance people need is not learning about Aboriginal Knowledge but in remembering their own.[126]

This memory has to be retrieved and retained through relationality:

The only sustainable way to store data long-term is within relationships—deep connections between generations of people in custodial relation to a sentient landscape, all grounded in a vibrant oral tradition . . . This doesn't need to replace print, but it can supplement it magnificently . . .[127]

In Aboriginal worldviews, relationships are paramount in knowledge transmission. There can be no exchange or dialogue until the protocols of establishing relationships have taken place. Who are you? Where are you from? . . .[128]

There is nothing remarkable about this, according to Yunkaporta. If anything, it is its opposite that is remarkable: 'It takes a dogged commitment to reductionism to ignore so many interrelated variables . . .'[129] This reductionism is what Yunkaporta defines as cultural immaturity, or 'silly thinking': 'Silly thinking is something everybody, myself in particular, is guilty of from time to time. It is forgivable as

---

125. Yunkaporta, *Sand Talk*, 157.
126. Yunkaporta, *Sand Talk*, 163.
127. Yunkaporta, *Sand Talk*, 167.
128. Yunkaporta, *Sand Talk*, 169.
129. Yunkaporta, *Sand Talk*, 184–85.

long as you're still listening.'[130] The practical lesson here is to avoid reductionism; to see things holistically:

> There's more to 'bush medicine' than what you might have heard along the lines of 'this plant was used by Aborigines to treat toothache' (always in the past tense, for some reason). It's about a way of living and a way of looking at the world, but above all a method of holistic inquiry.[131]

This perspective is all about 'how should we live?', but it does not start with that as an abstract question; it is neither instrumental nor rigorously analytical in its approach. How we should live emerges constantly out of remembering, storytelling, yarning—it occurs in the spaces between persons. And for Yunkaporta, anyone can do this.

> There are a lot of opportunities for sustainable innovations through dialogue between Indigenous and non-Indigenous Knowledge systems that might help civilisation transition into sustainable ways of living.[132]

Again, sustainability in this place, in these places, is a key concept for Yunkaporta. It may seem to be lost but is not. There is an inevitability to the resurgence of deep wisdom of the land:

> There are the old fellas who keep the original Law for us, holding it against the day of resurgence that will come. Those old fellas don't want to be written about or filmed . . . They have no need to assert or defend this Law. It is immutable and will outlast anything you can inscribe on paper or store on a server. This Law cannot be extinguished by the weak curses of land-use agreements and native title policies. This Law cannot be changed through dialogue either—it is the authority that shapes and regulates dialogue to keep it within sustainable patterns of creation. It is neither the irresistible force nor the immovable object. It is neither the action nor the reaction. It is the thing in between.[133]

---

130. Yunkaporta, *Sand Talk*, 186.
131. Yunkaporta, *Sand Talk*, 190–91 (but note Yunkaporta's concern about the inappropriate contemporary use of the term 'holistic', 185).
132. Yunkaporta, *Sand Talk*, 233.
133. Yunkaporta, *Sand Talk*, 246–47.

It is simply a matter of listening respectfully to these voices, of 'being like your place,'[134] and imagining different ways of seeing. 'Deep visualisation is like a poor man's virtual reality machine.'[135] Yunkaporta's book ends with a heartfelt cry for such deep imagining, and embarking on a journey of imagining.[136] For Australia, this could be a 'turnabout' event, a 'spark of creation like lightning when true learning takes place.'[137]

Much of what Yunkaporta has to say ventures explicitly into the traditional domain of theology, for example with regard to the nature of reality:

> First Peoples and Second Peoples, however, seem to have a fundamental disagreement on the nature of reality and the basic laws of existence. First Peoples' Law says that nothing is created or destroyed because of the infinite and regenerative connections between systems. Therefore time is non-linear and regenerates creation in endless cycles. Second Peoples' law says that systems must be isolated and exist in a vacuum, beginning in complexity but simplifying and breaking down until they meet their end. Therefore time is linear, because all things must have a beginning, middle and end. Aristotle invented that idea . . .[138]

Yunkaporta also addresses the nature of alienation from reality (that is, what Christian theology has traditionally called 'sin'). In Aboriginal stories, he writes:

> Emu is a troublemaker who brings into being the most destructive idea in existence: I am greater than you; you are less than me. This is the source of all human misery. Aboriginal society was designed over thousands of years to deal with this problem. Some people are just idiots—and everybody has a bit of idiot in them from time to time, coming from some

---

134. Yunkaporta, *Sand Talk*, 248–65.
135. Yunkaporta, *Sand Talk*, 255.
136. Yunkaporta, *Sand Talk*, 256–65.
137. Yunkaporta, *Sand Talk*, 111: 'Turnaround is an Aboriginal English word . . . creation events and times before the term "Dreamtime" was invented by settlers' (Yunkaporta, *Sand Talk*, 110).
138. Yunkaporta, *Sand Talk*, 51.

deep place that whispers, 'You are special. You are greater than other people and things . . .'[139]

All Law-breaking comes from that first evil thought, that original sin of placing yourself above the land or above other people.[140]

These statements come remarkably close to the traditional designation of *superbia* as the deadliest of the 'seven deadly sins' of mediaeval Christianity. *Superbia* is not quite the same as 'pride' in the way it is used, for example, by many of the writers in Anita Heiss's collection, where pride in one's people is closer to defiance in the face of two centuries of denigration (nor of course, does 'deadly' in 'deadly sins' carry the same connotations as in Australian Aboriginal English). Yunkaporta is reminding us of the danger of *superbia* in the classic theological sense.

Yunkaporta also asks some sharp questions about traditional understandings of the religious quest:

Adolescent cultures always ask the same three questions. *Why are we here? How should we live? What will happen when we die?* The first one I've covered already with the role of humans as a custodial species. The second one I've covered above, with the four protocols for agents in a complex dynamic system. The third is one, us-two will look at next.[141]

In other words, he does engage with these traditionally religious questions of theological anthropology, ethics and eschatology, but at the same time pronounces them to be 'adolescent' questions typical of immature cultures. Further, he does not raise them as abstract questions: these emerge from the stories. We need to acknowledge some explicitly theological appreciations of Indigenous spirituality, before moving on to distil some theological themes. I am not, however, going to venture into the territory of anthropological studies of traditional religion.[142]

---

139. Yunkaporta, *Sand Talk*, 30.
140. Yunkaporta, *Sand Talk*, 32.
141. Yunkaporta, *Sand Talk*, 102.
142. TGH Strehlow, *Central Australian Religion: Personal Monototemism in a Polytotemic Community* (Adelaide: Australian Association for the Study of Religion, 1978) is a classic work on this.

With Victor Steffensen we return to the notion of listening, but here it is listening specifically to how Aboriginal people have cared and continue to care for land. Like Yunkaporta, Steffensen's way of speaking is pervaded by a sort of animism that treats inanimate things as living beings. If we mistreat water, it will run away from us and hide;[143] isn't this exactly the story of the imposition of European land-use on country in Australia? European culture in Australia has been 'a culture . . . completely oblivious to land,' which has left the country like a house trashed by its tenants—so it is hardly a wonder the true owners recoil with profound grief, in all its manifestations, at what has been lost to them.[144] Fractured land leads to the fractured communities we see in contemporary Indigenous Australia.[145]

Victor Steffensen's book is all about land care based on proper use and management of fire. It is also the story of people who have known about this form of land care, but forbidden, for generations, from carrying it out. They have seen bushfires that they knew could have been prevented by the application of their traditional knowledge. He writes of his frustration at the way fire management has been carried out in Australia:

> No doubt we need firefighting equipment to fight fires and save lives and property, but we also need to look after the land too. Why isn't the subject of prevention and proactive measures being shared too? . . .
>
> Looking after the country with fire is a commitment that goes on forever into the future; it's not a program that is funded for three to five years and then stops. You can't have people burning country to funding guidelines rather than the right time for the country.[146]

Steffensen also welcomes the gradual change in attitudes that he now sees, among both Indigenous and non-Indigenous people:

> I remember times in the early 1990s when scientists would interview the old people about Indigenous fire knowledge.

---

143. Victor Steffensen, *Fire Country* (Melbourne: Hardie Grant, 2020), 54.
144. Steffensen, *Fire Country,* 86–87, 164.
145. Steffensen, *Fire Country,* 177, 180–81.
146. Steffensen, *Fire Country,* 86–87.

The old people wouldn't tell them much. Understandably, they didn't trust them with such information. Most of the time the researchers would leave thinking that the Elders knew nothing about fire at all.[147]

This is changing, according to Steffensen in his accounts of his own learning and teaching experiences, but needs to be managed well:

Teaching the fire knowledge in a public workshop was always going to be dangerous in many ways, but we can't exclude the white fella. We needed them on board too if we are going to put Aboriginal fire knowledge into the mainstream. We need to educate non-Indigenous people on the traditional fire as well, but in a way where Aboriginal people lead the process. Making sure the workshop focused on empowering Indigenous communities to run their own fire programs was key to sharing knowledge the right way.[148]

The philosophical issue for Steffensen—apart from the simple failure to listen to the wisdom of Indigenous people in Australia with regard to caring for the land—is analytical thinking, the method of thinking that splits instead of seeing everything together as a complex system.[149] It is this that gives rise to a divided mindset, and fragmented knowledge. It leads to people being disconnected from land, and from place. This is not a function of ethnicity or race: Steffensen draws the contrast not between 'black' and 'white' or Indigenous and non-Indigenous, but between connected and disconnected people.[150] Everyone was connected once, but many of us have lost our connections, and with it, our ability to think synthetically.[151] But place is filled with spirit, if we can discern it, and land has a voice, if we can but pause to hear it. This is true, says Steffensen, whether you believe it or not.[152] He is not concerned about belief as such; he is deeply concerned about the practical consequences of non-belief. Inability to hear the voice of the land and its traditional keepers has

---

147. Steffensen, *Fire Country*, 96.
148. Steffensen, *Fire Country*, 133.
149. Steffensen, *Fire Country*, 97, 197.
150. Steffensen, *Fire Country*, 163.
151. Steffensen, *Fire Country*, 97.
152. Steffensen, *Fire Country*, 162.

been disastrous in Australia, and Steffensen's book is a valiant attempt to put this situation right. It has to lead, however, to a combination of renewed practice and action—to 'praction,' as he calls it.

It is significant that these recent books by Steffensen and Yunkaporta both carry the subtitles, respectively, 'How Indigenous fire management could help *save* Australia' and 'How Indigenous thinking can *save* the world' (my italics). One claim is local and somewhat reticently in the subjunctive; the other is global and very assertively in the indicative. Indigenous voices are not all saying the same thing or in the same way—but notice that both of these are talking about salvation, which is a *theological* concept. It is one of the tasks of theology to speak of salvation, and another task of theology is to discern where the Spirit is moving, and therefore where salvation is to be found. Theology needs to listen to Indigenous voices, carefully and without interrupting, because this may be where the Spirit is moving in this country, in our time. This is why McKenna is correct in saying we stand at a decisive moment for the future. It is about well-being, not only of Indigenous people, but of all people who have made their homes on this country.

Theologies: The Rainbow Spirit Elders, Anne Pattel-Gray, Garry Deverell, Glenn Loughrey

In 1994 and 1995 Norman Habel, Robert Bos and Shirley Wurst convened a group of Aboriginal Elders, at their request, to formulate an Aboriginal theology. The resulting slim volume documents their conversations pointing to an Indigenous interpretation of the biblical writings. It is a rich source of ideas, but here I mention just two. First, the biblical story of Naboth's vineyard is once again prioritised—as a story of theft of ancestral land, by a powerful ruler, from a traditional custodian.[153] The prophet Elijah, often remembered largely for his passionate intolerance of local cults, here confronts and condemns the murder of Naboth and also the dispossession of his Indigenous land rights (I Kgs 21:1–19). This is the story in which we non-Indigenous Australians often fail to see ourselves as the beneficiaries

---

153. Nola Archie, Dennis Corowa, William Coolburra, Eddie Law, James Leftwich, George Rosendale, Jasmine Corowa (The Rainbow Spirit Elders), *Rainbow Spirit Theology: Towards an Australian Aboriginal Theology* (Melbourne: Harper Collins, 1997), 45–46.

of murder and dispossession. The second story concerns Abraham's understanding of the 'promised land' as a host country, in which settlement is to be negotiated in an ongoing process of agreement and mutual hospitality.[154] This picture of land use is contrasted to the more familiar story of Joshua as conqueror of land and dispossessor of its inhabitants. Concurrent with his work with the Elders, Norman Habel was developing a biblical theology of land, critically identifying a variety of land ideologies in the Bible, and greatly influenced by his conversations with Indigenous people, an Earth-centred reading of the biblical texts. This resulted in a multi-volume collection of essays known as the Earth Bible Project, which attempts to listen to the voices of the people of the land, the creatures of the land, and the land itself.[155]

An important book by Uniting Church theologian Anne Pattel-Gray appeared at the end of the 1990s. Although it does not address Indigenous issues to any great extent either theologically or in the light of Aboriginal world-views, it does express the sense of an Indigenous culture having been overwhelmed by what she calls 'the great white flood' of European immigration—flooded by something foreign, hostile and destructive. From the date of first settlement, the arrivals were unrelenting in their sheer numbers, an experience that also finds expression in Julie Janson's novel *Benevolence*. Added to this was the greed for land, the trees cut down and the herds of unfamiliar animals that devoured the grasslands. And then the attitudes of the new arrivals. Pattel-Gray's book is largely about racism in Australia, including the complicity of the Christian churches, both in the past and into the present. 'Racism,' she writes, 'is alive and well in Australia.' She aims to 'present the elements of this reality' and to 'address (it) by reviewing the historical and contemporary expressions of racism in society and in the church'.[156] Her book achieved its purpose at the time of its publication by confronting Australian churches with the implications of their own past actions, and inactions, in relation to Indigenous people.

---

154. Rainbow Spirit Elders, *Rainbow Spirit Theology*, 82–85.
155. Norman Habel, *The Land in Mine: Six Biblical Land Ideologies* (Minneapolis: Fortress, 1995); *Readings from the Perspective of the Earth*, edited by Norman Habel (Sheffield: Sheffield Academic Press, 2000); see also *Ecotheology*, volumes 5 & 6 (1998, 1999).
156. Anne Pattel-Gray, *The Great White Flood: Racism in Australia*. American Academy of Religion Cultural Criticism Series, Number 2 (Atlanta: Scholars Press, 1998), 1.

Like both Yunkaporta and Steffensen, Garry Deverell is uncomfortable with any sharp distinction between Indigenous and non-Indigenous: there can be no return to 'pure forms of pre-contact Indigeneity'.[157] And yet there is a way of being in and on country that needs to be recognised and whose insights need to be heard:

> Aboriginal identity is about the perseverance of a sense of Indigenous being—embedded in a deeply ontological sense of belonging to kin and country—over and against the will of a dominant culture and society that has systematically sought to erase these things . . . Aboriginality is most often preserved in the form of a memory and a deep-down sorrow pertaining to what has been lost or stolen—land, kin, dreaming—a sorrow manifested in various forms of grief and mourning, but also in the search for a justice in which these things might be returned or, at least, partially recovered.[158]

Deverell includes the personal story of what might be called a vision or mystical experience that underlies and informs his whole endeavour: the old people are present and waiting to be heard.[159] I have heard Murrundindi, the current Wurundjeri Ngurungaeta, tell of a very similar experience. Glenn Loughrey tells his own version of realising and being confronted by his own indigeneity.[160] Deverell also told this story in his Radio National interview on 20 September 2020, concluding with these words:

> I still don't know how to understand that experience . . . I tend to go with Aboriginal explanations of these things. We talk about a Dreaming, and the Dreaming is not the past; it's not mythology. The Dreaming is, if you like, something that's going on all around us and through us and beyond us at all times . . .[161]

---

157. Garry Worete Deverell, *Gondwana Theology: A Trawloolway man reflects on Christian Faith* (Melbourne: Morning Star, 2018), 19.

158. Deverell, *Gondwana Theology,* 49.

159. Deverell, *Gondwana Theology,* 17–18.

160. Glenn Loughrey, *On Being Blackfella's Young Fella: Is Being Aboriginal Enough?* (Melbourne: Coventry, 2020), 153.

161. Garry Deverell, 'The Bigger Picture: Indigenous theologian Garry Deverell on grounded spirituality', ABC Radio National, 20 September 2020 <https://www.abc.net.au/radionational/programs/soul-search/past-programs/> (accessed 22 September 2020). My transcription.

These are not isolated events; they are to be received with respect for those Aboriginal people who are willing to share them. They are events that are both historical (they can be documented and are located as having taken place in particular times and places), but they are also meta-historical (around, through and beyond us at all times). The theological question these experiences raises for me (and which I'd like to see Indigenous theologians explore) is this: would it be possible and legitimate to understand the incarnation and the resurrection, which are also located in time and place, but with meta-historical implications, as analogous to Dreamings?

The spirituality that arises from this perspective, however, is 'entirely about this world,'[162] entirely about caring for places and people, here and now. It puts some sharp questions to leaders of all the churches in Australia:

> Can any of you say . . . that you have truly taken responsibility
> for the wrongs your churches and congregations have visited
> upon the First Peoples of this land?[163]

Deverell speaks to the church and about the church in a way that encompasses all the churches: it is consistent with the worship of Aboriginal communities, which as Muriel Porter puts it, 'has refreshing internal integrity, and sits easily to a wide spectrum of Christian tradition. Ecumenism comes naturally . . .'[164] For Deverell, 'Dreaming' can be a source of God's revelation. This is a matter of theological epistemology. The Dreaming is 'like the presence of Yhwh in the burning bush,'[165] it is everywhere and always present. As Steffensen would put it, it's there whether you believe it or not. Theology is a search for truth, and the experience of First People is legitimate data for theological reflection: in fact this lived experience demands theological reflection.[166] It is this experience that calls, first and foremost, for 'telling of truth and . . . common ownership

---

162. Deverell, 'The Bigger Picture', 9.
163. Deverell, 'The Bigger Picture', 44.
164. Muriel Porter, *Land of the Spirit? The Australian Religious Experience* (Geneva: WCC/Melbourne: JBCE, 1990), 93.
165. Deverell, 'The Bigger Picture', 15.
166. Deverell, 'The Bigger Picture', 19.

of the undeniable truth of what has happened in this country.'[167] Reconciliation, if it is to happen, must begin with a confession of the truth. This is the only possible foundation for freedom (1 Jn 1:8) from the past, and this is essentially a *theological* task.[168]

At the heart of Deverell's book is his chapter on racism and the Trinity. At the outset he notes that Trinity Sunday often falls within National Reconciliation Week.[169] This opens a discussion of the relevance of the Christian doctrine of the Trinity to a respect for the essential equality of human persons. God is apprehended as a communion of love between three *personae*, conventionally and liturgically addressed as Father, Son and Holy Spirit. Deverell puts these names in inverted commas, an acknowledgement that this naming (though by no means the substance of the doctrine) has been called in question in recent decades, especially by feminist theologians. The substance of the doctrine is an affirmation of equality, within the Godhead. Deverell discusses the scriptural texts on Wisdom and Word (referring to the second trinitarian person) and Spirit (the third person). In the second person, God gives us a representation of Godself, here and now. The third person, 'more wild and mysterious in her workings, like a wind that comes from nowhere and goes to nowhere,' brings truth, hope and joy.[170] This trinitarian notion of God is essentially a story:

> A story of God, and God's dealings with the world of human beings that unleashes the power to transform our despair into joy, our hearts of stone into hearts of flesh and feeling. The doctrine of the Trinity is shorthand, in other words, for everything the Christian faith has to offer by way of truth, justice, faith and hope. It is the grammar out of which we may start to comprehend our world, our society and our church as the arena of God's action for forgiveness, justice and peace. It is the divine *mythos* through which we might answer even the most puzzling of our human questions.

---

167. Deverell, 'The Bigger Picture', 42.
168. Deverell, 'The Bigger Picture', 43.
169. Deverell, 'The Bigger Picture', 51. National Reconciliation Week takes place annually between 27 May (the date of the 1967 referendum) to 3 June (date of the High Court Mabo decision). Trinity Sunday is a moveable feast, tied to the date of (western) Easter.
170. Deverell, 'The Bigger Picture', 53.

God is a communion of love, a God who makes Godself vulnerable, and the giver of life and all the vitality that goes with it. The most puzzling question Deverell brings to this reality is: why racism? It isn't enough simply to say 'racism is evil because human beings are equally deserving of respect and care, whatever their ethnicity' because this is not at all axiomatic: we can still ask the question 'why?'—a question 'many Australians find much more difficult to answer . . . (not that we ask ourselves the question very much at all)'.[171] This assertion of human equality must have a logical foundation if it is to be taken as properly fundamental, and the logic of this has to be a *theological* logic:

> In the face of Christ, we learn that God is no bully, but prepared to come amongst us in the vulnerable form of the Son, to remonstrate and plead with us, that we might choose the way to life . . . Racism is evil because God the creator is a communion of love since all eternity, and wants to include everyone, without remainder . . .'[172]

None of this lets the Christian churches off the hook. The following chapter is addressed to Deverell's Indigenous sisters and brothers, and it's about how to relate to the church, a church—or rather a collection of churches—that has worked in close collaboration with the state in 'this nation's most original sin: the dispossession of its First Peoples and the genocidal policies that remained in place for close to 150 years.'[173] Churches that have not yet begun, except in the most tokenistic ways, the work of self-emptying love. How, Deverell asks his First Nations kin, ought we engage with such a church? There are three alternatives. There is the way of denial—denial, that is, of one's own Aboriginality, 'pretending you are something you are not'.[174] But 'denying who you are is no path to salvation . . . Resist as though your life depends on it. Because it probably does.'[175] The second way is that way of anger and despair. Anger offers a sense of pride in identity, and for a Christian there can be an appeal to the example of Jesus himself. Deverell gives a long quote from Matthew 23 to support this position.

---

171. Deverell, 'The Bigger Picture', 54.
172. Deverell, 'The Bigger Picture', 54–55.
173. Deverell, 'The Bigger Picture', 62.
174. Deverell, 'The Bigger Picture', 65.
175. Deverell, 'The Bigger Picture', 66.

But, 'there is a shadow side to anger'.[176] It is seductive, but it burns and consumes, and becomes ultimately self-defeating. The third, least fashionable, way is in the end the only way—it is the maturity to speak truthfully, but in love. It is to 'grow up into Christ' and it is expect a 'mature, grown-up church'.[177] The chapter finishes with a reflection of Jesus' encounter with the Indigenous Canaanite woman in Matthew 15, an encounter in which Jesus himself had to grow up beyond the limited worldview of his own tribe.

Reconciliation, if it is real, creates responsibility.[178] Deverell calls for alterations to 'the power-structures of the church in a root-and-branch manner,'[179] and for worship that 'that looks and sounds like it comes from *this* country and not another'.[180] Almost half of Deverell's book is devoted to detailed recommendations for Indigenous Australian liturgy, liturgy replete with invocations of the God of our wisdom and calls for hearts that can feel.

Glenn Loughrey's *Another Time, Another Place* is a collection of six sermons that address what the author sees as the elements needed for renewal of the church in Australia. Though Loughrey writes from an Anglican perspective, his concern, like Deverell's, is for the renewal of the church in its widest, ecumenical sense. The first step will be to let go of the old imported model from Europe, 'breaking the pot' in which gospel has arrived, so it may be planted in this new, unfamiliar soil. This, he warns, is not to be done naively, with undiscerning adoption of Aboriginal spirituality and language, as this runs the risk of appropriating Aboriginal intellectual property.

He outlines four elements of what needs to follow. The first is truth-telling about the history of the church in Australia. Here he sees the Statement from the Heart as carrying a similar challenge to the church as the Royal Commission into Institutional Child Abuse. Both concluded with their reports in 2017, and both 'shifted the balance of power out of the hands of the institution and into the hands of the general public, especially, in these cases, the victims of the failures of these institutions'.[181] While the church experienced a narrowing of its

---

176. Deverell, 'The Bigger Picture', 68.

177. Deverell, 'The Bigger Picture', 69.

178. Deverell, 'The Bigger Picture', 40.

179. Deverell, 'The Bigger Picture', 63.

180. Deverell, 'The Bigger Picture', 29.

181. Glenn Loughrey, *Another Time, Another Place: Towards an Australian Church* (Melbourne: Coventry, 2019), 17.

sphere of influence in public life, its quest for the justice of God has paradoxically also expanded because of global alliances of like-minded people. The second element is engagement with the surrounding culture and space, which is predominantly the secular culture of the Enlightenment. Loughrey reminds us that the colonisers came to Australia 'with little or no religious guidance . . . and were left to their own imaginations to create meaning in the new world'.[182] One effect of this secularity is that Australians, rather than being socialised into religion early in life, often begin to discover it only later in life. The third element is coming to terms with the language and spirituality of this place. Place is given its Indigenous significance here, though Loughrey notes the 'sensuous brutality deeply fixated with the human engagement with place' in Second People Australian art, and a concomitant sense of having been defeated by place.[183] Although he notes a certain basic quest for authenticity ('be fair dinkum') and equity (the 'fair go') in the colonialist culture, it does not yet attain the ability to live in harmony with the land.[184] It distrusts authority, including that of the church. Yet it still seeks to dominate the land. The fourth element, then, is the need for maturity, both as the nation and the church. Loughrey, in full agreement here with what we have heard from both Yunkaporta and Deverell, puts it this way:

> Maturity places us where we understand that what we wished for, what we were told and who we are, are three completely different experiences . . . It happens when we put aside what we wished for in childish hope; it happens when we are okay with the disparity between these and the reality we experience every day.[185]

> Maturity is the strength to engage with the unknown without the need for assurance that all will be well.[186]

The end of these four stages is transformation through 'relationships and love but not in a warm fuzzy way; it is confrontational and transformative.'[187]

---

182. Loughrey, *Another Time*, 27.
183. Loughrey, *Another Time*, 33.
184. Loughrey, *Another Time*, 35.
185. Loughrey, *Another Time*, 41.
186. Loughrey, *Another Time*, 44.
187. Loughrey, *Another Time*, 50.

Loughrey's more recent book, *On Being Blackfella's Young Fella* covers many of the same 'geophysical' themes as Yunkaporta, often citing his book, as well as questions raised by some of the other writers considered above. In some ways, this book fits better in the 'ge-ological' section of this essay, along with Yunkaporta and Steffensen. There are the same ideas of multiple levels of sovereignty and citizenship, of kinship understood as open kinship, of the interconnectedness of all reality, of country not simply as passive space or commodity, but as the dynamic fulness of all its inhabitants. There is, however, a logic to considering Loughrey's works together, even though this book is not so explicitly theological.

It is a disturbing book, for a number of reasons. It starts with an acknowledgement of country that goes beyond the conventional words you'll hear at any citizenship ceremony: 'I also acknowledge that this land was stolen and those who stole it have no intentions of giving it back any time soon.'[188] It ends with the seemingly uncompromising statement 'We do not need Christianity . . . we do not need a saviour or an intervening god'[189]—the 'we' meaning Aboriginal people: 'We do not need salvation . . . We are Aboriginal/That is all we need to be'.[190] A strange thing, you might think, to hear from an Anglican priest. In between the beginning and the end is an extended account of the author's growing up in a farming family totally in tune with the land they were working but prevented from buying the farm because of the exclusion of Aboriginal people from civic life in Australia prior to 1967. As if all this were not disturbing enough, there is the added discomfort about how this book came to be written: a public dialogue with a well-known Iona hymn writer, ostensibly about connections between Aboriginal and Celtic spiritualities, but hijacked, the author felt, by a focus on Celtic Christianity instead of Celtic spirituality.[191] Even well-meaning whitefellas, it seems, can get caught up in the domination game, perhaps even without realising we're doing it. The author wakes at night thinking 'that perhaps, just perhaps, that there is no such category as Aboriginal spirituality'.[192]

---

188. Loughrey, *On Being*, 5,
189. Loughrey, *On Being*, 151.
190. Loughrey, *On Being*, 155.
191. Loughrey, *On Being*, 11.
192. Loughrey, *On Being*, 21.

Loughrey rejects the term 'religion' and expresses discomfort with 'spirituality', at least in its popularised, consumer-oriented packaging. In some ways his book sounds like an uncompromising rejection of theology, but let's not jump to that conclusion too quickly: the reality for Loughrey may be more complex. Essentially this book is the account of Loughrey's search for his own identity, both Anglo-Australian and Aboriginal Australian (and Anglican within that mix):

> The question that troubles me most personally is why I find myself in this place where I have to hold in tension the two ways of seeing. It would be so much easier to be one or the other.[193]

So what are we to make of Glenn Loughrey's apparent rejection of Christianity, or better, the word 'Christianity'? The context is his protest against the common view of 'Aboriginals as people of deficit,'[194] and the Christianity he rejects is one that endorses such a view, one that suggests Indigenous people need to be saved, from themselves. Consequently, Loughrey rejects a particular understanding of atonement, the Anselmian idea of a sacrifice to expiate the sins of the world:

> Our culture resolved relationship or kinship problems and the problems of human failings here and now without the need for a sacrifice to set us free. That idea is barbaric to us.[195]

Indeed, Anselm's view of atonement may well have made sense in the context of eleventh-century England, and the old Anglo-Saxon practice of payments to expiate wrongdoings; in fact we could see it as a brilliant piece of contextual theology in its time and place. It makes less sense in contemporary Australia, and it is by no means the only understanding of 'salvation' or even 'atonement' within the tradition.[196]

---

193. Loughrey, *On Being*, 153.
194. Loughrey, *On Being*, 150.
195. Loughrey, *On Being*, 151. See also Charles Taylor, *A Secular Age* (Cambridge MA: Belknap, 2007), 78–79 for the role of this understanding of atonement in the emergence of secularism.
196. Gustav Aulen, *Christus Victor: An historical study of the three main types of the idea of the Atonement*, translated by AG Hebart (London: SPCK, 1970) is the classic treatment of this theme.

Loughrey acknowledges that the spirit world is not necessarily benign, that there is need for protection and direction at times—he does not reject the need for salvation.[197] His hesitations about 'spirituality' are also well founded, as this term denotes, in the secular west, a privatised, often commercialised and 'intrinsically trivial'[198] quest for well-being that has little to do with the overwhelmingly terrifying sense of presence encountered in some of the biblical narratives.

Loughrey's *On Being Blackfella's Young Fella* may be a disturbing book, but it is not an angry book. Rather, it's a book that grapples deeply, painfully and honestly with the experience of being pulled between two aspects of personal identity, living immersed in and being fully part of two different cultures, whose protocols and priorities, thoughtforms and even languages for encapsulating reality are so differently aligned. Above all this book is about an Aboriginality that, in Deverell's words, 'is most often preserved in the form of a memory and a deep-down sorrow pertaining to what has been lost or stolen— land, kin, dreaming'.[199] What we hear in this book is something of that deep-down sorrow, a sorrow that sits in unresolved tension with the equally deep sense of calling to follow Jesus, and to ministry in his name: 'Becoming Anglican was one of the whitest things a blackfella could do,' Loughrey writes. 'Being an Anglican priest was and is the ultimate sign of assimilation . . .'.[200] Loughrey has written in his earlier book about his faith and his sense of church, and how these need to find authentic *Australian* expressions. His sincerity about these things is not to be doubted. The later book is about his Aboriginality. The central point he makes is that the Australian Indigenous worldview is a 'philosophy of enough, enough not as a deficit but as sufficient'.[201] This is a message we need to hear as Christians and as Australians, and indeed, as human beings in the twenty-first century. It will demand some sacrifices from us, intellectual sacrifices of long cherished assumptions, about the world, ourselves and our faith. Or at least, about how our faith is expressed. The one who stands at the centre of our faith is still there, but he may just surprise us by starting to look a bit more Aboriginal.

---

197. Loughrey, *On Being*, 31.
198. Taylor, *A Secular Age*, 508.
199. Deverell, 49.
200. Loughrey, *On Being*, 25.
201. Loughrey, *On Being*, 97.

A Forum for Theology in the World Vol 7 No 2/2020

Elements of a Theological Appreciation

The aim of offering a theological response is definitely not to impose yet another Eurocentric grid over all that has, hopefully, been heard in the preceding discussion of Indigenous writing. Rather, this is an attempt to connect the deep wisdom inherent within these Indigenous voices with the deep wisdom I believe to be buried within the stories and teachings familiar to theological scholarship. Part of the problem is that these teachings, like the systems of western church governance, are themselves expressions of linear, analytical and systematising ways of thinking, or at least are interpreted as such. Theology has a tendency to make statements: affirmations, confessions, creeds, all of which define the limits of acceptable belief. These condense and attempt to make consistent the variable testimonies of the canonical texts. They are necessary to take account of the complex breadth of scripture, of what I have called its polyphony, and to reject any sectarian tendency to take one or another of scripture's statements and amplify it as some sort of one and only criterion of truth. The philosopher and physicist Carl Friedrich von Weizsäcker explains the concept of heresy in exactly these terms: 'heresy (*hairesis*) is to take (*hairein*) on a partial truth from the whole of the Christian truth and make this part absolute.'[1] Credal and confessional statements are in fact 'agreed statements', products of debate and emerging consensus arrived at over time and through the collective wisdom of many minds. They are, however, by nature reductionist to some degree. They, and the theological systems built around them, are useful as compendia, but the problems of applying logic too rigorously to belief

---

1. *CF* von Weizsäcker, *The Relevance of Science: Gifford Lectures 1959–1960* (London: Collins, 1964), 179.

and worldview are well known. The pearl of great price can be lost in the argumentation, the bargaining between parties, the talk without listening. For this reason it is important to look to the resources of what Norman Habel calls the 'green texts' rather than the 'grey texts,'[2] and what Dietrich Ritschl calls 'best part' of the tradition.[3] There is also a place for statements of appreciation for whatever is good (Phil 4:8) and for what the Holy Spirit might be saying to us through those whom we encounter and their worldviews.

The theological critique of religion and secularism

Dietrich Bonhoeffer speaks of a theological criticism of religion, a 'freedom from religion,' and an emerging Christianity that will be 'religionless'. What he was objecting to was a whole host of ideas and practices: religious jargon, reliance on a God invoked as 'the apparent solution of insoluble problems,'[4] and indeed, some of the frontier pieties that Indigenous writers describe being inflicted upon Indigenous people. These are not new ideas. Christian theology has worked in the shadow, or perhaps in the light of Bonhoeffer's criticisms for almost seventy years. God speaks to us not in our weaknesses, 'not at the boundaries where human powers give out,'[5] not to our deficits, but in our strengths and our self-reliance as human beings. Bonhoeffer shares Glenn Loughrey's rejection of deficit thinking.

Dietrich Ritschl traces this deficit idea of humanity in general back to Augustine: 'Western theology has taken from Augustine the theological license to separate divine grace from the world and from history, and that means from nature.'[6] This leaves western thinking with notions of original sin—especially with regard to a humanity

---

2. Norman Habel, *An Inconvenient Text: Is a Green Reading of the Bible Possible?* (Adelaide: ATF, 2008).

3. Dietrich Ritschl, *Memory and Hope: An inquiry concerning the presence of Christ* (New York: Macmillan, 1967), xv, 226. Though this expression is used only twice in this book, at the beginning and end, the concept lies at the heart of what Ritschl is seeking to achieve here.

4. Dietrich Bonhoeffer, *Letters and Paper from Prison*, 3rd edition (London: SCM, 1971), 280–86, here at 281 (Letters to E Bethge, 30 April and 5 May 1944).

5. Bonhoeffer, 282. *Letters and Paper from Prison* was first published in English in 1953.

6. Ritschl, *Memory and Hope*, 127. See also James Boyce, *Born Bad: Original Sin and the Making of the Western World* (Melbourne: Black Inc., 2014).

that might be considered in a 'state of nature'. This is exactly how the Europeans of the eighteenth century regarded Aboriginal people, who were thus also considered to be separated from God's grace. This also involves a static view of God: 'God is no longer seen as the God of the Exodus, who moved with his people through history . . . but rather God is understood statically'.[7] Ritschl, like Loughrey, is also uncomfortable with the term 'Christianity', preferring the terms *Christus praesens*, or '"God in Jesus Christ," but not "Christianity"'.[8] Ritschl made the point that 'Theologians are not keepers of archives but interpreters of the present in the light of God's history with his people in the past'.[9] Ritschl's words, written more than fifty years ago, are an explanation of what Loughrey is doing and saying: God encounters us in our strengths, as Bonhoeffer also taught us, and in our self-confidence in whom we are, not in our deficiencies.

There are, of course, risks in this process of focussing on the 'best part' of the tradition. First, what criteria are to be applied to discerning what is the 'best part'? Second, are we not very close here to the concept of heresy mentioned above? In answer to both questions Ritschl highlights the centrality of story:

> Stories can express things for which other idioms would be inappropriate. In particular the identity of an individual or a group can be articulated by stories. People are what they tell of themselves (or what is told to them) in their story and what they make of this story.[10]

Much of what we have considered above has been the telling of personal and communal stories. Some Indigenous thinkers considered here have sought to bring these stories into critical dialogue with the biblical stories and theological traditions. In this dialogue, some of the biblical stories will draw attention to themselves more prominently than others. These will include some texts that will strike us as being more offensive than we had previously realised, and

---

7. Ritschl, *Memory and Hope*, 131.
8. Ritschl, *Memory and Hope*, xxii, footnote 2; 186.
9. Ritschl, *Memory and Hope*, 68.
10. Dietrich Ritschl, *The Logic of Theology: A Brief Account of the Relationships Between Basic Concepts in Theology*, translated by John Bowden (Philadelphia: Fortress, 1987), 19.

other texts that will affirm elements in what we are told by Indigenous people. Their stories become contextual criteria, in this country, for us in our reading of the Bible and the tradition.

Ritschl also draws a helpful distinction between what is 'of lasting importance' and what is 'of momentary urgency':

> We meditate on, pray about and discuss what is 'of lasting importance' in tranquillity, whereas we fight for what is 'of momentary urgency' because for the most part we have already become guilty and are already too late for the fight. The church which devotes itself only to what is 'of lasting importance' loses the present and fellow human beings; anyone who turns only to what is 'of momentary urgency' loses the question of God and the legitimacy of his or her argument.[11]

> We can learn from the Biblical writers that the question of *right* and *wrong* is less important than the question of what is *urgent*.[12]

Ritschl reminds us that Christian theologians very often come 'too late for the fight': we find ourselves trying desperately to assuage our guilt by playing catch up to other forms of social commentary.

Kathryn Tanner says something similar about timing:

> making a decision about proper action or belief seems less a matter of application of explicit precept and more a matter of tact and good timing—knowing when and where a certain affirmation or deed is called for ... Something like a sense for the game, a feel for the possibilities of Christian living.[13]

This 'sense' or 'feel', she says elsewhere, depends on socialisation into a tradition: the theologian must 'know the theological tradition of which he or she is a part'.[14]

---

11. Ritschl, *Logic*, 89.
12. Ritschl, *Memory and Hope*, 194.
13. Kathryn Tanner, *Theories of Culture: A New Agenda for Theology* (Minneapolis: Fortress, 1997), 81.
14. Kathryn Tanner, *God and Creation in Christian Theology: Tyranny or Empowerment?* (Oxford: Blackwell, 1988), 168–69.

One element in identifying the 'best part' of the tradition is the freedom to distinguish between what Norman Habel calls the 'grey' and the 'green' texts of scripture. This is a distinction Habel developed in his work on the biblical hermeneutics of ecotheology, but it is applicable to other areas of discussion. In the attitude to the earth in the Bible we are faced with a conundrum. In Genesis 1:26-28 we find the command to human beings to 'subdue and have dominion' over the earth—the original mandate for empire. In Genesis 2:15 we find an alternative account of the purpose of human life: in relation to Earth (Habel capitalises this as a proper noun and leaves out the conventional definite article), where the earth creature, the *adam*, is given the task and purpose, the vocation, in the primordial garden to 'till it and keep it'. But even this, according to Habel, is a mistranslation, coloured by the earlier mandate.[15] We should be translating the mandate in Genesis 2.15 as 'to serve and preserve'. To *serve* the land, that is to act as a servant to the land and care for it; to *preserve* country and look after it. This is a custodial, conservationists' role, but more than a role—it is a purpose for living. It is a vocation for being human that precedes the better-known callings of the Abrahamic religions. We still have the hermeneutical problem as to which of the callings, Genesis 1 or Genesis 2, to prioritise. The distinction acknowledges that there are 'grey' texts that are ecologically unhelpful, but also discovers 'green' texts like Genesis 2:15 that had previously, for various reasons, gone unnoticed. Given the connection between kin and country outlined by Deverell, we can extend Habel's theme of care for land to care for the people (human and non-human) of that land. Indeed, Habel himself makes exactly this connection.[16]

What Indigenous writers, both theologians and non-theologians, are telling us are home truths that the church in its widest sense, and the nation, need to hear and respond to, in timely and appropriate ways. The church needs to do this just to carry out its calling to be church, on this country. I am not suggesting we reject terms like 'religion' and 'Christianity', any more than a term like 'culture'. I am

---

15. Norman Habel, *An Inconvenient Text: Is A Green Reading of the Bible Possible?* (Adelaide: ATF, 2009), 65–77. See also *The Earth Story in Genesis: Earth Bible 2*, edited by Norman Habel and Shirley (Sheffield: Sheffield Academic Press, 2000).

16. See 'The Adelaide Declaration on Religion and the Environment', especially points 2 & 3, in *Ecotheology*, Nos 5&6 (1998–1999): 255–56. This agreed statement was drafted by Norman Habel.

simply suggesting we refrain from making idols of them. These are complex terms, and we need to ask what it is that causes people at times to react against them. And nothing in the theological critique of religion should blind us to the equally powerful theological critique of secularism, with its reductionist worldview and its logical consequence of lonely disconnected selves.[17]

Waiting and urgency

At this point we are in a position to rediscover some ideas in the Christian theological tradition, or rather revisit them—as if reading them for the first time, in the light of our listening to Indigenous voices. What follows is my own personal response, my side of the yarn. It attempts what I call an appreciation of Indigenous voices, a careful listening. Theologians are trained to read and listen critically. In this appreciation I attempt to suspend the usual critical, judgemental, function of theological thinking, and attend to the things we need to hear in the stories we are told, not losing sight of the things of lasting importance but prioritising the things of momentary urgency, here in this country, now in the third decade of the twenty-first century. The awareness of things of lasting importance remains, as a safeguard against what might at any time appear to be of momentary urgency. Afterall, there have been theological justifications in the past, seen as necessary at the time, for slavery and racism, and the imperial project was itself once seen as a God-given opportunity for evangelism. Listening in an attitude of appreciation to Indigenous voices may sharpen our critical faculties in reappraising such moments in the history of the church and its theological reflection. This essay attempts to be a listening and an appreciation–a listening for what is good. The various questions posed in the rest of this chapter are questions for ongoing discussion.

It would not be at all surprising if there were things Indigenous people didn't want to share: after all, they live with the experience daily of almost two and a half centuries of not being listened to. But there clearly are things they want to tell the rest of us in this country: the sheer volume of recent Indigenous writing in Australia is testimony to this. They want to tell us not just for their own benefit, but for ours

---

17. Charles Taylor, *A Secular Age* (Cambridge MA: Belknap, 2007).

as well, and above all, for the benefit of country. The 'rest of us' is the 'we' in the title to this essay—non-Indigenous Australians in general, but with particular attention to those inclined to reflect theologically on matters of faith and ultimate meaning.

Genuine mutual understanding emerges from dialogue, and this takes time and an appreciation of culture and cultural differences— including the length of time, the duration of waiting required, the continuum that Geert Hofstede calls the long-term orientation of a culture.[18] Hofstede applies this mainly to Confucian-influenced cultures, but Australian Indigenous cultures know themselves to be of even longer duration:

> Remember that our lived culture is the oldest on this planet and that the ancestors go back much further; therefore, they take a long view of life and responsibility.[19]

This is a network of responsibility that applies, whether we know it or not, to all of us who live on country. Indigenous Australian cultures value waiting respectfully, to listen before speaking, to be invited before arriving. I have experienced this waiting with my colleague Sid Graham, a Kaurna man visiting his wife's Ngarrindjerri country at Raukkan, in South Australia: we waited at the gate of the local cemetery till a family visiting a grave several hundred metres away had finished their visit and come out of the cemetery. Only then did we go in. I am grateful for the advice given by Wurundjeri woman Woterang, calling on participants in a recent webinar to wait, if possible, for a welcome by local people whenever and wherever travelling anywhere in Australia.[20] Glenn Loughrey explains the need for this welcome to country, and its relationship to the prior condition of acknowledgment of country.[21] Yunkaporta speaks about sitting and

---

18. Geert Hofstede, <https://geerthofstede.com/culture-geert-hofstede-gert-jan-hofstede/6d-model-of-national-culture/> (accessed 6 July 2020). See also my 'Bakhtin on the Nature of Dialogue: Some Implications for Dialogue between Christian Churches,' in *Temenos: Nordic Journal of Comparative Religion*, 49/1 (2013): 65–82.
19. Glenn Loughrey, *On Being Blackfella's Young Fella: Is Being Aboriginal Enough?* (Melbourne: Coventry, 2020), 145.
20. National Reconciliation Week webinar organised by student leaders at Camberwell Girls Grammar School, Melbourne, 28 May 2020.
21. Loughrey, *On Being*, 146–147.

waiting to be invited, as the preparation for real listening. Waiting to be invited in is precisely what we European settlers/invaders in Australia failed, and still fail, to do.

Waiting is also in no way foreign to the biblical worldview: 'how long must we wait' is a common theme in the Psalms. The world had to wait for the coming of the messiah. The church calendar includes a season focussed on waiting, the time of Advent. This, and not just the messianic side of Advent, is a theme that deserves attention. Respect calls for appropriate waiting in some situations. But this does not override the prior call for the truth-telling that needs to be done without delay.

Truth

Bruce Pascoe calls for a 'true conversation about what has been lost and what gained, and how that has forged the schizophrenic national psychology' of Australians.[22] Truth telling is a major theme of Mark McKenna's book.[23] Although truth-telling is of lasting importance, they both insist that the particular truth-telling under discussion here must now be considered a matter 'of momentary urgency'. Chris Budden and Garry Deverell both make theological points out of it: 'reconciliation begins, as the Johannine traditions says, with a confession of the truth.'[24] The Statement from the Heart is, among other things, a call for truth-telling. Truth is a theological concern, and theology attempts an act of naming the truth (another reason why names and naming are theologically important). We have to start with truth-telling, because this provides the methodological basis for the appreciation we are attempting.

There are several aspects to this matter. The first is relatively simple: it is the truth-telling that Pattel-Gray, McKenna, and Pascoe all call for. The truth about Australian history, and the church's role in it, has to be told and received honestly. There has to be truth-telling not just about the past but about the present as well. We know deaths

22. Bruce Pascoe, 'Temper Democratic, Bias Australian,' in *Salt: Selected Stories and Essays* (Melbourne: Black Inc, 2019), 57–65, here 65.

23. Mark McKenna, *Moment of Truth. Quarterly Essay 69* (Melbourne: Black Inc, 2018), 15ff.

24. Garry Worete Deverell, *Gondwana Theology: A Trawloolway Man Reflects on Christian Faith* (Melbourne: Morning Star, 2018), 43.

in custody happened in the past, but what of the death in police custody of Yorta Yorta woman Tanya Day in December 2017? How can this still be happening in the twenty-first century? Without the acknowledgement of truth, there can be no reconciliation.

There is a second area in which the call for truth-telling is essential. Theology is a search for truth, and needs to start from truthful interpretation of its own sources. Part of truth-telling is to acknowledge the 'grey texts' of scripture, including those stories that undergird an imperial mindset. It is true that the stories of Joshua's warlike conquest of land tend to override and negate the stories of Abraham's negotiations and agreements with the local people among whom he lives, to say nothing of his bargaining with God on behalf of the inhabitants of a local city (Gen 18:22–33). It is true that Elijah's criticism of Ahab for dispossessing Naboth of his ancestral land looks less noble when set beside the prophet's vehemence against the local Indigenous prophets (1 Kgs 21:1–24; 1 Kgs 18:30–40). But it remains the case that both types of story are included in the same canon, and Elijah's opposition to the prophets of Baal may make more sense in context than the blatant intolerance it may, on the face of it, seem to suggest. More importantly, it remains the case that the overwhelmingly dominant story in the Hebrew scriptures is a story of liberation from slavery.

There are grey texts as well as green texts in holy scripture: grey texts that justify conquest and slavery and exploitation and even war crimes and genocide. They are there in the text, and we have to acknowledge that they are there. We also have to assert that biblical hermeneutics is not a closed enterprise, and that new interpretations of these texts are constantly being opened for debate.[25] We are not tied to uncritical readings of ancient texts, however sacred, nor past interpretations. We also have to look for the polyphony of sacred scripture, that includes the green texts that may lie hidden and unexplored, texts that speak of justice and care for, and indeed participation in all creation. These are texts we need to bring to the

---

25. An example of this rethinking of textual meanings from the local context but another area of debate is the ATF Press series on sexuality: *Five Uneasy Pieces: Essays on Scripture and Sexuality*, edited by Nigel Wright (Adelaide: ATF, 2011); *Pieces of Ease and Grace: Biblical Essays on Sexuality and Welcome*, edited by Alan Cadwallader (Adelaide: ATF, 2013); and *Kaleidoscope of Pieces: Anglican Studies on Sexuality*, edited by Alan Cadwallader (Adelaide: ATF, 2106).

table as prophetic correctives to conquest and exploitation. The point remains valid, however, that the grey texts need proper scholarly exegetical treatment. The fact remains that these texts are parts of the canon and have been used in justification of the colonial project. It is a matter of truth-telling that our purposeful and respectful and honest listening to Indigenous voices should bring these texts to light.

There also has to be an honest acknowledgment of the problematic of secularist ideology. This is the worldview of the European Enlightenment, which shows its influence on Australian culture, both Indigenous and non-Indigenous, in numerous ways. This is simply a matter of truth-telling. It is also a matter of truth that, as Deverell put it, 'deep down, many Australians do not believe that the ethical injunction against racism is absolute'.[26] This is a truth that must be taken with utmost seriousness and confronted unceasingly. The question remains: can we hear, tell and live with the truth about our colonial history? Can we act in accordance with this truth, to bring about a just settlement in this land? What can we do about it?

Place and Abiding Events

'We need non-Aboriginal Australians,' writes Bruce Pascoe, 'to love the land'.[27] The writers surveyed all speak, in one way or another, of the importance of place, specific places. Dreaming or Abiding Events are always located, in places. A person's identity is determined by the place of their conception or birth. Swain outlines a whole ontology of place in Australian Indigenous thought. Abiding events endure, whether you believe them or not, in specific places. This observation makes Val Plumwood's call for a decolonisation of geographical names all the more significant. The imposition of European names misrepresents the landscape, to the point of falsification, as Loughrey points out:

> I grew up on the top of a song-line—the Great Dividing Range. It is not a divider, but a connector . . . just as the Great Barrier Reef is not a barrier . . .[28]

---

26. Deverell, *Gondwana Theology*, 54.
27. Pascoe, 'Sea Wolves,' in *Salt*, 115.
28. Loughrey, *On Being*, 123.

Contrast this to the way places were and continue to be viewed by Second Peoples in Australia. We can point to the problematic of the central Cartesian distinction between subject and object. Contemporary Australia is uncritically wedded to this distinction, and the analytical thinking that goes with it, in which the primary existing thing is the thinking (and observing, gazing, analysing, and possessing) subject; all else is what Descartes called 'extension,' out there—to be objectified and treated as something ultimately either for 'improvement' or exploitation. This is the disjunction identified by the radical orthodox theologians between '(epistemological) object over (teleologically indeterminate) subject,'[29] which in turn excludes or marginalises patterns of knowledge based on participation in community, or in other words, the sorts of Indigenous knowledge that Yunkaporta and Steffensen both speak about.

Theology in Australia needs to explore the scriptures and the tradition for vestiges of the God who loves places and chooses to dwell in a particular place. The Hebrew scriptures know a God who chooses a dwelling place in the Ark of the Covenant, and on Mount Zion. The Christian tradition has stories of holy places—Jerusalem, Assisi, Sergiev Posad are all holy places for many Christians. The late Davis McCaughey once told a story about accompanying a group of Russian Student Christian Movement members to the holy island of Iona, and his surprise when, on making landfall, they fell to their knees in reverence for the *place*. Places, in this view, gain an aura of God's presence from those who have worshipped there, as TS Eliot hints:

> You are not here to verify,
> Instruct yourself, or inform curiosity
> Or carry report. You are here to kneel
> Where prayer has been valid.[30]

We need to be wary of the emotional impact when we close down or close off or destroy places that have gained such an aura, and to which

---

29. John Milbank, Graham Ward, Catherine Pickstock, 'Introduction: Suspending the material: the turn of radical orthodoxy', in *Radical Orthodoxy: A New Theology* (Routledge: London/New York, 1999), 17.
30. TS Eliot. 'Little Gidding', in *Collected Poems 1909-1962* (London: Faber and Faber, 1963), 215.

people have built up such a connection. An English hymn begins: 'we love the place O God, wherein thine honour dwells . . .'[31] Can we imagine the sense of frustration and humiliation of being locked out of sacred sites, places that have been of deep significance to our own people for generations, and which are integral to care for country? This is not a trivial sentiment.

There can of course be a theological objection to the sacralising of place. In John 4:20–21 Jesus appears to negate any hallowing of a particular place: 'the hour is coming when neither on this mountain nor in Jerusalem will you worship . . .' This sentiment inspired the secularisations of particular places during the Reformation and received a further boost from the Enlightenment to which we owe what Charles Taylor calls our sense of the 'buffered self'. This, like Steffensen's 'disconnected people', is the notion of self that stands alone in sharp distinction from the world around us, in contrast to the 'porous self' that takes its sense of identity from connection to kin and country. The pre-modern 'enchanted world', according to Taylor, 'in contrast to our buffered selves and "minds", shows a perplexing absence of certain boundaries which seem to us essential.'[32] In that older world, meaning does not reside simply in human minds, but 'is already there . . . quite independently of us; it would be there even if we didn't exist. And this means that the object/agent can communicate meaning to us, impose it on us . . . By bringing us as it were into its field of force.' That older sense of object, agent and place was not extinguished from the 'social imaginary' of Europeans till the late eighteenth century,[33] according to Taylor; that is, till about the time Arthur Phillip was hoisting the union jack at Sydney Cove. This insight does not negate Jesus' words to the Samaritan woman in John 4, but it might lead us to read them differently, and in ways that allow us to think again about how we treat Indigenous sacred sites.

Secular Australia has, of course, its own sacred places. Australia is a country full of war memorials, most of them dating from immediately after World War I, and some of them explicitly evoking a spirit of empire.[34] They date from a time when Australians were

---

31. *Hymns Ancient and Modern*, Standard Edition (London: William Clowes, 1916), number 242.
32. Charles Taylor, *A Secular Age* (Cambridge, USA: Belknap, 2007), 33.
33. Taylor, *A Secular Age*, 208.
34. The war memorial (1929) at Camperdown, Victoria, is explicit in this evocation.

British subjects, and a majority non-Indigenous Australians identified as children of empire. Even when empire is not directly mentioned, the colonial fantasy (Maddison) lurks within the wording. 'God, King and Country' is a frequent word combination, associating God with empire and nation, the specific Australian commonwealth that had come into existence as a federation of self-governing colonies barely a decade before the war. These monuments have been added to subsequently to memorialise other conflicts in which Australia has been involved. The colonial mentality, which received a boost during the great war, a reversion from the optimistic (white Australian) nationalism that had led up to federation, is never far away. Significantly, very few if any of these monuments memorialise the frontier wars of the very long nineteenth century.[35]

If we are to think critically about this civilisation at a deep level, as Yunkaporta in particular asks us to do, we have no alternative but to think theologically. This history and this theology raise the question: Can we move from understanding 'country' simply as national identity, to country as Country in the way this word is used in Indigenous welcome to Country ceremonies? Can we move from the 'King and Country' of the war memorials, where country means nation, to the 'Kin and Country' that Garry Deverell places near the centre of his thinking, in which Country means land, in the fullest sense, and belonging? And how might theology help us make this transition? With regard to abiding events, is it possible Christians have read into the biblical narrative an overarching lineal structure that may not really be the most important structure; that we may have missed the turns and returns, the goings out and the comings in that suggest a far more complex view of history.

Interconnections

Several of the writers considered speak of knowledge conserved and passed on by personal, one-to-one 'yarning'. Reality is something communicated between persons, with proper respect for persons. This

---

35. From 1804 to 1928, for this purpose. See Jens Korff, <https://www.creativespirits. info/aboriginalculture/history/australian-aboriginal-history-timeline/ massacres> (accessed 4 July 2020). Even this list of massacres fails to recognise Indigenous deaths in custody, deaths that resulted from the Maralinga nuclear tests, or the current high incidence of Indigenous youth suicide in Australia.

respect between persons is the opposite, in Yunkaporta's view, of the 'original sin' of putting oneself before or above others. Unfortunately, western civilisation shows a whole history of doing just that–putting ourselves, and our much-vaunted civilisation, above others and the cultures of others. A consequence has been our arrogance in Australia of ignoring Indigenous care for land, for country, and for particular places on country. And yet we find something similar in the Christian tradition: the first shall be last and the last first. Is this merely a pious wish, or a symbolic order for the choreographing of ecclesiastical processions? Or is something more demanded of our attention?

With the aid of Indigenous thinking, let us track this idea to its source: the possibility that reality may be ultimately personal, an event that takes place between persons, in interpersonal relationships. Again, we can connect this possibility, as Garry Deverell has done, to the way this understanding is manifest in the Christian tradition: the trinitarian notion of God. The doctrine of the Trinity is essentially an attempt to say just one thing: that ultimate reality (that is what Christians call God) is personal and interpersonal. This is the point that Immanuel Kant famously failed to understand. 'From the doctrine of the Trinity, taken literally, nothing whatsoever can be taken for practical purposes', he wrote,[36] perhaps because at the time the doctrine of the Trinity had become so much an accepted formula that its significance was no longer greatly understood, even perhaps by those who affirmed it. But it is the nature of traditions to bear witness to truths, even in times 'when the word of the Lord (is) rare . . . (and) visions . . . not widespread' (I Sam 3:1). Kant lived at a time when there was a dearth of understanding of this particular concept. He was right perhaps in saying it was not useful, in the sense that it did not lend itself to being used *instrumentally* to assert or achieve some sort of control over nature. But, as Garry Deverell has shown, Kant was wrong in suggesting it has no practical implications. We have no such excuse: there has been an immense work of rediscovery and revival of trinitarian thinking and its implications over the last forty

---

36. 'Aus der Dreieinigkeitslehre, nach dem Buchstaben genommen, läßt sich schlecherdings nichts fürs Praktische machen'. Immanuel Kant, cited in W Kasper, *Der Gott Jesus Christi* (Mainz: Grünewald, 1982), 320, footnote 167. Unless, or course, Kant means emphasise 'literally' as opposed to metaphorically.

years or so.[37] Reality, in this framework, is made up of persons and their personal relationships, and in a plural way: it is neither singular nor merely dual. Yunkaporta uses a dual pronoun very effectively to convey the intimacy of a conversation between 'us both'. But 'both' can be self-enclosed: three opens up plurality.[38] Jürgen Moltmann has demonstrated how trinitarian thinking about God, and the trinitarian invocation of God, embodies a critique of monarchical or imperial notions of God.[39]

Here we need to consider a text that may be 'grey', if not in itself, then possibly in relation to our consideration of Indigenous worldviews. We need to look closely at the notion of kin, which according to Deverell is 'deeply connected with our (i.e. Indigenous) spirituality of land'.[40] Kinship, which is an important theme in some of the Hebrew scriptures and indeed in much of Christian popular culture, is deeply problematic in the New Testament. In Mark 3:31–35 Jesus appears to reject his family and establish a new community that will take the place of ties of kinship. This sentiment is repeated even more strongly in Luke 14:26–27. The implicit critique of kinship in these passages needs careful study, with the question to be asked: Is this a rejection of Indigenous kinship ties, or is it rather a rejection of obstacles within Jesus' own historical and social context to what he called 'the kingdom of heaven'? How is Jesus' critique of kinship to be understood in relation to the fifth commandment, to honour one's mother and father? Glenn Loughrey points to a possible answer when he highlights Jesus' controversy in Mark 7:1–23 as an example of 'elder-abuse', thus modifying the critique of kinship earlier in the gospel.[41] Part of the problem in Australia may be that we Second Peoples are descendants of those who left behind their families of origin, their kin, and their places of indigeneity. Our attitudes to

---

37. I would date this revival from 1980, the publication of the German original of Moltmann's *Trinity and the Kingdom of God: The Doctrine of God* (London: SCM Press, 1981).

38. This is the logic of Athanasius' argument that the Spirit is divine, fully a person of the Trinity, because the Spirit opens the possibility of human participation in God. See JND Kelly, *Early Christian Doctrines* (London, Adam & Charles Black, 4th edition 1968), 257–58.

39. Moltmann, *Trinity and the Kingdom of God*, 129ff. and 191ff.

40. Deverell, *Gondwana Theology*, 14.

41. Glenn Loughrey, *Another Time, Another Place: Towards an Australian Church* (Melbourne: Coventry, 2019), 34.

homeland can be very different from that of people who have not emigrated.[42]

We need also to consider the possibility that Jesus was reacting against a closed understanding of kinship, very different from the open kinship relationships that Indigenous writers speak about. Another possibility, in other words, is to refuse to see this critique in terms of the either/or dichotomies so favoured by western thinking, but to follow Yunkaporta's 'us-two' framework. This may allow us not to oppose these two mandates to one another, but to search for how they connect. We can note that Jesus' criticism of loyalty to family comes within the context of a call to a universal commonwealth of inclusion and mutual responsibility, which according to Deverell is not in any way alien to Indigenous thinking.[43] Within this universal sphere of responsibility, there are more specific and concrete responsibilities to our neighbour, the person closest to us, the person next to us. These responsibilities are governed by protocols as to how to encounter strangers, people from outside our immediate group: the dialectics of invitation and respectful acceptance, of safety and responsibility for guests. These protocols are a major theme of Tony Swain's book. Respect is a constant theme in Indigenous writing and speaking, self-respect as well as respect for others. We need also to take into account the connection between people and country, including personal identity and country. In the light of this connection, we can see Indigenous understandings of kinship to be a function of the relationship to land. In a theological perspective, kinship comes under the same mandate as care for land.

There is another issue at stake here, and once again it touches on the heritage of the Enlightenment. This is the emergence, mentioned above, of the 'buffered self' in place of what Taylor calls the porous

---

42. An example of a different sort of European attitude finds expression in a comment by an acquaintance of mine who lives in Moscow, speaking of the thirteenth-century prince, St Daniil: 'he is in the ground here and he is also with God, and he prays for us.' See my 'Language of the Heart,' in *Meanjin* 65, 4 (2006): 212–21, here 218. Garry Deverell suggests that Indigenous perspectives might help Second Peoples find their own connectedness: 'The Bigger Picture: Indigenous theologian Garry Deverell on grounded spirituality', ABC Radio National, 20 September 2020 <https://www.abc.net.au/radionational/programs/soul-search/past-programs/> (accessed 22 September 2020).
43. Personal conversation 9 July 2020.

self. Taylor is in agreement with Yunkaporta that 'something . . . has taken place in our civilization . . . But the problem is defining exactly what it is that has happened.'[44] He is in agreement with Pascoe in acknowledging 'the secular age is schizophrenic, or better, deeply cross-pressured'.[45] When I hear Indigenous people speak about the Dreaming, I hear something very similar to what theology recognises as the communion of saints, an interconnectedness and a porosity of the self that is independent of time. Persons are formed in interconnected community. This is the truth affirmed in what might otherwise seem the rather abstract doctrine of the Trinity: that reality is ultimately like this interconnection; and so much so that God can be spoken of not simply as a God who loves, but *as love itself* (I Jn 4:8, 16). This interconnected love not only binds people and families and communities together but, as Stan Grant has pointed out, negates all the conventional markers of identity. In this he has the support of no less a figure than St Paul (Rom 10:12; Gal 3: 28; Col 3: 11; and, of course, 1 Cor 12: 30–13:13). Persons are essentially porous to one another; this is the opposite of the 'solitarist identity'[46] so common, unfortunately, in non-Indigenous Australia.

Sovereignties

Mitri Raheb offers a succinct summary of the components of empire, and how this overlaps with the notion and reality of colonies. These components are: control of movement; control of resources; settlements; state terror; exile; control of holy places; and an imperial theology:

> A highly important aspect of the matrix of control that empires exercise is the construction of new colonies or settlements or cities built on conquered land with the express purpose of controlling the native people and all natural resources.[47]

---

44. Taylor, *A Secular Age*, 426.
45. Taylor, 727. See also Taylor, *A Secular Age*, 594–605 for a discussion of what he means by 'cross-pressured'.
46. Stan Grant, *On Identity* (Melbourne: Melbourne University Press, 2019), 79.
47. Mitri Raheb, *Faith in the Face of Empire: The Bible Through Palestinian Eyes* (Bethlehem: Diyar, 2014), 62.

The applicability of this to the European colonisation of Australia hardly needs explanation. The writings considered above all refer to the controls exerted over Indigenous people in Australia with regard to movement, resources, the exile of people from their own lands and sacred places until relatively recently, and the state terror still demonstrated by the large numbers of Indigenous people in custody.

Mitri Raheb proposes four existential questions he believes the colonised must continue to ask. First: where are you, God? Note that this question is in the vocative. It is not the question of the European Enlightenment about (the existence or non-existence of) God: it is a question addressed *to* God. Second: Who is my neighbour? In other words, who may I trust, and who must I assist? The similarity with the Indigenous concept of kin hardly needs stating. Third, what is the way to liberation? Fourth: When will we have a state? In the Australian context, this can be taken to mean when will we have Mark McKenna's 'more complete commonwealth'.[48]

Chris Budden, as we have seen, understands sovereignty as based in and shaped by covenant. It is therefore not something simply handed over by God, 'not power entrusted to secular authorities'.[49] Sovereignty is always subject, whether it acknowledges this or not, to God, and there can be various overlapping sovereignties operating within a society. If sovereignty is ultimately God's, then it is power expressed relationally—for the reasons we considered above: the trinitarian understanding of God sees God as more like a community of persons than simply something like a person. The problem is that states tend to understand sovereignty *simply* as power. Modern atheism serves two social interests, according to Budden: it removes the possibility of a sovereignty of God that might modify national claims to sovereignty; and it negates (in practice if not always quite in theory) the insight that human beings might be related to others and owe their existence to others. I am grateful to Sandy Yule for a further comment on this question:

> On the theology of sovereignty, I am remembering the classic study by H Richard Niebuhr, *Radical Monotheism*. Absolutist despotism is an example of what he calls 'henotheism', that is,

---

48. McKenna, 75ff.
49. Chris Budden, *Why Indigenous Sovereignty Should Matter to Christians* (Adelaide: MediaCom Education, 2018), 56.

the deification of some created being into the place of God. Our Australian sense that to accept Aboriginal sovereignty over the land is to destroy the sovereignty of parliament needs to be challenged as an idolatry of parliament. We could talk in terms of 'authority' here. The 'voice to parliament' in the Statement from the Heart explicitly recognizes the authority of parliament! The authority of parliament should not expunge the authority of Aboriginal voices over what affects Aboriginal people, just as it does not expunge the voices of citizens more generally.[50]

Again, the point is that the sovereignty of God, if explicitly or even implicitly acknowledged in the constitution of a nation, modifies, at least in theory, any absolute claim to sovereignty. Absolute sovereignty in this perspective is idolatry, the substitution of something created in the place of God. Thus, despite there being some truth in atheist criticisms of Christianity (of which Nietzsche continues to be the most articulate exponent), Budden's remark carries weight: 'I still think that the loss of God better serves those with power than those without.'[51]

This is not the only way of modifying a claim to absolute sovereignty: the Geneva Conventions and the various United Nations declarations make similar claims to take precedence over the absolute claims of nation-states in relation their own citizens or residents. In any case, sovereignty is multifaceted and multilayered: different sovereignties co-exist within any political system. The Statement from the Heart acknowledges the sovereignty of the Australian Commonwealth and of Parliament, but it reminds us of an older, pre-existing (and still existing) set of sovereignties. What the Statement rejects is the suggestion that the sovereignty of the Australian Commonwealth nullifies pre-existing sovereignties.

The other point Budden makes is that 'claims to sovereignty are inherently claims about salvation, the issue of what human well-being looks like and how it is claimed'.[52] They are, in other words, about the reign (or more conventionally, the 'kingdom') of God, the state

---

50. Sandy Yule, personal communication, 13 July 2020. The reference is to H Richard Niebuhr, *Radical Monotheism and Western Culture, with Supplementary Essays* (London: Faber, 1961).
51. Budden, *Why Indigenous Sovereignty*, 88–89.
52. Budden, *Why Indigenous Sovereignty*, 19.

of being in abundant life into which we as human beings are invited. And sovereignty is not a unitary phenomenon, it is multifaceted and plural. Different sovereignties can and do co-exist in the same place. The path to salvation is reconciliation—with God, with country, between peoples.

This has implications for Loughrey's struggle with identity, a struggle that he expresses on behalf of many of the contributors to Anita Heiss's book. Here I need to quote Amin Maalouf, a thinker who has wrestled with similar questions with regard to his own Arab-French identity, and who points out:

> Anyone who claims a more complex identity is marginalised . . . But by virtue of this situation—peculiar rather than privileged—they have a special role to play in forging links, eliminating misunderstandings, making some parties more reasonable and others less belligerent, smoothing out difficulties, seeking compromise. Their role is to act as bridges, go-betweens, mediators between the various communities and cultures.[53]

Such individuals who struggle to accept and live with their own complex inter-cultural identities will, if Jesus is to be believed, be called children of God (Matt 5:9). Maalouf makes it clear that this is no easy space to occupy, but it is essential for the future of the world that there be such people who do consciously occupy it and refuse to be pressed, ordered or bullied (even, or especially, by the well-intentioned) into one or another simple, one-dimensional identity. Identity doesn't have to be a badge to be proud of, or a cuirass to be worn to confront others, but rather a heritage of belonging to share with those whom we meet, and which may even give us points of contact with others. Maalouf recommends 'a new approach to the idea of identity' in which

> Identity would then be seen as the sum of all our allegiances, and, within it, allegiance to the human community itself would become increasingly important, until one day it would become the chief allegiance, though without destroying our many individual allegiances.[54]

---

53. Amin Maalouf, *On Identity*, translated by Barbara Bray (London: Harvill, 2000), 4, 6.
54. Maalouf, *On Identity*, 84.

Complexities of citizenship and the sense of belonging will necessarily correspond to the complexities of sovereignties. The reality of overlapping sovereignties has practical implications for how significant places are treated. The destruction at Juukan Gorge highlights a difference between the law of the nation and lore of the land. An act of this sort goes beyond a tension between what is legal (according to the law of the nation) but not quite ethical. It is about more than the inevitable damage to the reputation of a company or industry or nation; it is indicative of something diseased at a deep level in the soul of the nation.

Pathways to transformation

Theology also has something to say about the path to transformation. Moses was given a sense of purpose at the burning bush, to set his people free—a task that would involve his setting out on the pathway to a confrontation with a powerful ruler and all the imperial and theological apparatus that supported that ruler's power. The people Moses set free also had a pathway to follow, to live in a covenant relationship with their God. The earliest disciples of Jesus had a pathway simply to follow him wherever he went, for, as Peter said, 'you have the words of eternal life' (Jn 6:68). On occasions the disciples' pathway was to be sent out to carry out acts of healing and liberating. Christians are called to continue to follow these pathways to transformation, and this is essentially a practical task. What unites Christians, according to Kathryn Tanner, is 'nothing internal to the practices themselves . . . (but) concern for true discipleship, proper reflection in human words and deeds of an object of worship that always exceeds by its greatness human efforts to do so'.[55] Clarification of this discipleship is 'more likely to come out of wrangling with others about its nature', and is reason in itself for 'the ongoing practice of choosing dialogue over monologue'[56]—for continuing to yarn, in other words.

We have seen that Victor Steffensen's book is also the story of people who have known about Indigenous land care but have been forbidden from carrying it out. They have seen bushfires they know

---

55. Kathryn Tanner, *Theories of Culture: A New Agenda for Theology* (Minneapolis: Fortress, 1997), 152.

56. Tanner, *Theories of Culture*, 174–75.

could have been prevented by the application of their traditional knowledge. We need to exercise our imaginations once again at this point: can we imagine the sense of frustration and humiliation at seeing newcomers ignore what we know, or the ongoing shame we might feel at having failed to protect our ancestral lands? The message that comes out in Steffensen's book is that this has been and continues to be a matter of vocation, that is, of the purpose for living, the reason for which people are here, on country, and alive. The other side of this coin is that the frustration of a fundamental reason for being is inevitably going to lead to existential crisis: why continue to live if the task you've been given is denied you, if you have literally nothing to live for? The high incidence of suicide among young Aboriginal people in Australia should, under these circumstances, not surprise us, but should definitely shock us to the core. I'm reliably told that youth suicide is not an element in traditional Indigenous societies, so why is it so common now, and why in remote communities, even where there is an ongoing connection to land?

Nearly all the contributors to Anita Heiss's collection speak of their pride in being of this or that Indigenous descent. Many of them are people who were separated from their families of origin and have lived a long time without knowing their ancestry, so pride in their discoveries is understandable. But maybe pride alone is not quite enough. Certainly it's important to give young people a solid confidence in who they are, in their identity, but then let them do what most young people want to do—to go out and get to know other young people, generally young people who are different from themselves. This may mean the opportunity to leave remote communities, at least for a while. It does not have to mean assimilation so long as it does not erase identity in the sense of belonging, but rather builds on a solid confidence in such identity, a solid sense of who you are. Let's remember that identity is always multi-layered and more complex than we might be tempted to think.

The Australian national anthem claims that 'we are young and free'. But with an ageing population and, in world terms, one of the older federal constitutions, this claim seems somewhat hollow. Do we act like a nation that has yet to grow up? There are two questions embedded in Yunkaporta's words. First, Do we live in what McKenna calls an incomplete commonwealth, because—as Yunkaporta suggests, but without quite saying it outright—we have not yet grown beyond a certain cultural immaturity? The weight of all the writing considered here suggests the answer is Yes. All the writers considered are saying, in one way or another, that our maturity as a nation will be conditional on recognition of Indigenous sovereignty and our wider Australian immersion in the Indigenous wisdom about how best to live in this land. By this I mean that we will have not merely read, marked and learnt but most importantly, also inwardly digested this Indigenous wisdom, so that it has become an integral part of who we are, as Australians. Second, these resonances push us to explore our maturity of faith: once again, how we interpret the scriptures in all their polyphonous richness, how we worship with a liturgy 'that looks and sounds like it comes from *this* country and not another,'[57] and how we live respectfully on this land—treating it as no less holy a place than the land promised to Abraham and his descendants. This is the maturity to 'grow up in Christ'.[58] Maturity involves respect: Indigenous writers say a great deal about respect. The well-being not only of Indigenous people, but all people in Australia, is diminished by the current unreconciled reality. Ultimately, well-being is what Christians call salvation.

---

57. Deverell, *Gondwana Theology*, 29.
58. Deverell, *Gondwana Theology*, 69.

Conclusions

Kate Grenville's Mrs Macarthur expresses with tragic honesty the predicament of all Second Peoples in Australia:

> I am a newcomer here, ignorant of the inner grain of the place . . . Still, newcomer though I am, this is home to me now. Any other place would be exile . . . I have to face the fact that I am a thief . . . (and) underneath that goodwill, we all know an undigestible fact: I am not prepared to gather up my children and get on a ship and return to the place of our forebears.[1]

Being Australian is problematic. We are, most of us, living on someone else's land (without paying rent, or paying it only on our terms), and many of us, not just Indigenous Australians, are conflicted about different aspects of our identities ('from all the lands on earth we come'). Our listening to Indigenous voices calls us, Australians who may or may not also be Christians, to revisit and think about certain elements deeply embedded in our own traditions: truth-telling, place and its significance, personal interconnection as the pattern of ultimate reality, sovereignties, and pathways to life in its abundance. It calls Christians to think theologically, and to act and advocate strongly and unapologetically for the realisation of these elements. This calls the church to explore new ways of being church in Australia. It calls Australia to explore new ways of being Australia. Through the bulk of this essay I have tried to listen to practical experience, in the form of Indigenous voices, and move from that to theological reflection. Now I want to reverse that direction: to start from theology, and recommend some practical applications, for us, here and now.

---

1.   Kate Grenville, *A Room made of Leaves* (Melbourne: Text, 2020), 314.

The ten commandments have been mentioned several times, and there are two elements in them I would like to highlight. One is the commitment to kin, in the fifth commandment. In both versions of this commandment, we should note that commitment to kin is tied to security and longevity *in the land* (Exod 20:12; Deut 5:16). Kin and country are not separated here. This is about acknowledging where we have come from, and the people from whom we have come. It is also about acknowledging and being at home in our own cultures—even when we non-Aboriginal people may have left our parental homes and lost contact with our roots in other lands. It may be 'that when we connect with those roots, we will understand our place in Australia better'.[2] This may sound paradoxical, but it is in line with what Yunkaporta asks of us, to examine our own culture. For Christians, there is an added reason for knowing our own cultures, and that is simply that Jesus did exactly this. In Luke's Gospel (Lk 2:41–52) we have a picture of him drinking in exactly his ancestral culture. It is in his total confidence about his own culture that the gospel narratives show him constantly crossing and re-crossing all manner of cultural barriers. Examples are too plentiful to need mentioning here.

The biblical genealogies begin with an act of (reciprocal) hospitality: Sarah and Abraham in the desert visited by three strangers (Gen 18:1–15).[3] And another of the commandments, the fourth, records the commitment to the sabbath rest, which—again, in both versions—is offered as a day of rest to animals and also to the stranger within the gates (Exod 20:10; Deut 5:14). The latter version explicitly records why the stranger should be included in the day of rest, in terms of where the locals, the ones offering hospitality, had come from: slavery, the bottom of the social pile, in an alien place. How close does this come to many of us 'Second People' in Australia:

> From distant climes, o'er wide-spread seas we come,
> Though not with much éclat or beat of drum,
> True patriots all; for be it understood,
> We left our country for our country's good.[4]

---

2. Sandy Yule, personal communication, 24 August 2020.

3. The reciprocity, and interconnectedness, of hospitality in the biblical narratives is explored by Thomas Naumann, 'Gastlichkeit: Biblische Dimensionen', in *Gastlichkeit: Eine Herausforderung für Theologie, Kirche und Gesellschaft*, edited by Ulrike Link-Wieczorek (Leipzig: Evangelische Verlagsanstalt, 2018), 55–79.

4. (Possibly) Henry Carter, 'True Patriots All' (1801): <https://www.australianculture.org/prologue-true-patriots-all-1801/> (accessed 25 August 2020).

Hardly surprising that the locals found us barbaric. The sabbath commandment demands hospitality to the stranger, because we also were once strangers—certainly in this country. For Christians, once again, this injunction is amplified by the example of Jesus. In Matthew 2:13–18 we see the infant Jesus as a refugee, or rather an asylum seeker, in Egypt of all places—the last place a Jewish family would normally seek refuge (they'd been there before, after all). In John's Gospel we hear that he came to his own, but his own did not receive him (Jn 1:11). Jesus knew the experience of exile and counteracted it by the general invitation to hospitality: 'Come all who labour and are heavy laden' (Matt 11:28). This is to say nothing of the hospitality at the heart of the central act of Christian worship, the eucharist.

There is one other element in the biblical traditions that these reflections highlight, and that is the hallowing of particular places. Let me cite just one emblematic example: Jacob, in the desert, on the run from his murderously angry brother and afraid, wakes from a dream and exclaims: 'Surely the Lord is in this place and I did not know it . . . How awesome is this place! This is none other than the house of God, and this is the gate of heaven' (Gen 28:16). Can we see that maybe the Lord has been in *this* place for a very long time, and *we* (non-Indigenous Australians) did not know it? Again, Jesus seeks out deserted places for his encounters with the God he calls 'father'. Like Jacob's encounters, this is often a struggle, and as with Jacob (Gen 32:24–30), the desert is always transformed into a place of blessing. The conversation with Samaritan woman mentioned above does not desacralise place—on the contrary, it acknowledges every place to be a point of potential encounter with the holy, a place of Abiding Events. The Earth Bible Project is an extended attempt to value Earth and all its interconnected living communities as such a place of blessing and encounter. What practical wisdom can we draw from these brief theological reflections?

To my non-Indigenous theological colleagues, I would say this. We are the best equipped in this country to see through the hard binaries of the living and the dead, of this reality or another possibility, and to perceive that the deepest and most important truths find their best expression in story and metaphor. We are best equipped to discern the moments of transparency in the membrane between this solid reality of times and places and things, and other (possible) dimensions of reality that may even escape such limits. We are the best equipped to begin to understand what our Indigenous friends are talking about, because—in theory if not always in practice—we are most free of the 'dogged commitment to reductionism' that Yunkaporta speaks about, the constraints imposed, albeit with the best of intentions and admittedly with many impressive outcomes, by the European Enlightenment. I am in no way questioning the genuine benefits of this Enlightenment heritage, but simply pointing out that it comes at a cost. It has limited our access to other ways of knowing, and the cost of these limits is gradually becoming more apparent to our post-modern world. Many in our society have been left feeling, exactly as Nietzsche had predicted, with far less solid ground under their feet. So, why have we been so quiet? It's not because we've been listening to voices from our own country. There are some notable exceptions, like Chris Budden and Marion Maddox, but in general we've been very good at listening to the great minds of Europe and America, and for a few of our number, to voices from Asia. The new crop of Indigenous writing in this country is inviting us to a conversation; this essay is just a very small contribution. We can start to listen, and we can try to hear, and we can begin to take part in the conversation into which our Indigenous friends are inviting us.

To conclude this conversation, this yarn, I want to offer my fellow non-Indigenous Australians three suggestions about how we might start to listen to this land and its people. I don't claim to be an expert on any of this, or even particularly good at it, so these three suggestions are as much to myself as to anyone else. Nor do these suggestions take the place of the recommendations we have heard here from Indigenous writers themselves.

First, I suggest we adopt the new understanding of identity, and our own complex identities, suggested by both Amin Maalouf and Stan Grant. This would a first step towards welcoming strangers and practising hospitality. It may also be a first step towards our own maturity.

Second, I suggest we Second Peoples make friends with our own heritage cultures, whatever they are, and no matter how much we know or don't know about them. 'You can't understand other people's stories if you don't understand your own.'[5] Not everyone knows

---

5. Mathangi Subramanian, *A People's History of Heaven* (London: One World, 2019), 280.

where they've come from—I get that—and even if we do, none of us can ever know more than a few tiny fragments of insight into the lives of others, even those of our own parents, let alone any further back. But we all have stories. I'm not suggesting we go visiting our imagined ancestors, fossilised in amber at some arbitrary point in the past. But let's remember them as real people, with whom we may not necessarily agree, but real people with hope and fear, passion and courage:

> The foot that quits its native glen
> With half unwilling motion,
> Shall mount with dauntless courage then
> The Bark that braves the Ocean.[6]

A romantic sentiment, maybe, except that the courage continues in all those who have come and continue to come to this country by boat. And let's also get to know our heritage cultures as a living cultures—learn their languages, sing their songs, and keep in touch, if we know them, with our living relatives, wherever they live. If we are fortunate enough to be descended from more than one heritage culture, we have the privilege and the responsibility to be bridge builders between cultures. The world needs such bridge building now more than it ever did in the past (read what Amin Maalouf has to say about this). We don't have to idealise our heritage cultures—we have to be honest, but also charitable. Our ancestors may not have seen the world as we see it, and in fact undoubtedly saw it otherwise, but we can at least try to understand their perspectives. This reconnecting to origins is potentially dangerous, if it were to lead us into some new sort of idealisation of those origins—identity in the sense Stan Grant rightly rejects. It is not for its own sake, this reconnection, but for us to understand ourselves anew, not as separate, disconnected individuals or buffered selves, but as human beings connected to the rest of the human community, the life community and the land from which we emerge and to which we return. Reconnecting is a first step in this process.

---

6. 'The Emigrant Highlander's Wife' (words by John Marriott, 1807). Track 3 on compact disc *Curious Caledonians*, by Evergreen Ensemble. ABC Classics, 2019. <https://www.evergreen-ensemble.com> (accessed 18 September 2020).

Third, I suggest we make friends with the places where we live. This is our place, but only insofar as we are its temporary custodians. We need to look after these places for whomever might live here after us. And for the non-human creatures who share them with us now—these are their places as well. If this particular place of ours has a traditional language or a culture associated with it, we could attempt to get to know its traditional owners and custodians, and seek a welcome to this place, but always bearing in mind and carrying through the precondition for such a welcome—a proper acknowledgement of traditional ownership and custodianship. Let us learn something of their language, or at least something of their way of seeing this place and the world. This has practical implications for Australians. How can we live on this country without seeing it simply as empty space, and without the need to 'disturb the earth' by digging it up? It has practical implications for Christians in Australia: we know about holy places, but how can we begin to see the holiness of *these* places and *this* country? How might an acknowledgement and an inner perception of the Dreaming, or Abiding Events, not threaten but inform and deepen our faith in the God of Jesus Christ? Let us look for connections to country, mindful of the Abiding Events deep in the ground beneath our feet. This reconnecting is a first step towards living on country and in this place respectfully.

Selected Bibliography

Non-Fiction

Archie, Nola; Dennis Corowa; William Coolburra; Eddie Law; James Leftwich; George Rosendale; Jasmine Corowa (The Rainbow Spirit Elders), *Rainbow Spirit Theology: Towards an Australian Aboriginal Theology* (Melbourne: Harper Collins, 1997).

Arendt, Hannah, *On Violence* (New York: Harcourt, Brace and World, 1969).

Aulen, Gustav, *Christus Victor: An historical study of the three main types of the idea of the Atonement*, tr. AG Hebart (London: SPCK, 1970).

Balabanski, Vicky, 'An Earth Reading of the Lord's Prayer: Matthew 6.9-13,' in Norman C Habel (ed.), *Readings from the Perspective of Earth* (Sheffield: Sheffield Academic press, 2000).

Bonhoeffer, Dietrich, *Letters and Paper from Prison*. 3rd edition (London: SCM, 1971).

Boyce, James, *Born Bad: Original sin and the making of the western world* (Melbourne: Black Inc., 2014).

Brett, Mark, *Decolonising God: The Bible in the Tides of Empire* (Sheffield: Sheffield Phoenix Press, 2008).

Brett, Mark, *Locations of God: Political Theology in the Hebrew Bible* (Oxford University Press, 2019).

Brett, Mark and Naomi Wolfe, 'Sovereignty: Indigenous Counter-Examples,' in *International Journal of Public Theology* 14 (2020), 24–40.

Budden, Chris, *Following Jesus in Invaded Space: Doing Theology on Aboriginal Land*. Princeton Monograph Series 116 (Eugene, USA: Pickwick, 2009).

Budden, Chris, *Why Indigenous Sovereignty should matter to Christians* (Adelaide: MediaCom Education, 2018).

Busch, Eberhard, *Karl Barth: His life from letters and autobiographical texts*, tr. John Bowden (London: SCM, 1975).

Byrne, Frank (with Frances Coughlan and Gerard Waterford), *Living in Hope* (Alice Springs: Ptilotus, 2018).

Clark, CMH (Manning), *A History of Australia*, vols I–VI (Melbourne: MUP, 1963ff.)

Clark, CMH (Manning), *Occasional Writings and Speeches* (Melbourne: Fontana, 1980).

Cole, Keith, *Groote Eylandt Pioneer: A Biography of the Reverend Hubert Ernest de Mey Warren, Pioneer missionary and explorer among the Aborigines of Arnhem Land* (Melbourne: Church Missionary Historical Publications, 1971).

Chryssavgis, John, 'Mere History or Mystery: the story of the Desert,' in Graeme Ferguson and John Chryssavgis, *The Desert is Alive: Dimensions of Australian Spirituality* (Melbourne: Joint Board of Christian Education, 1990).

Courtney, Adam, *The Ghost & the Bounty Hunter: William Buckley, John Batman and the theft of the Kulin Country* (Sydney: ABC Book 2020).

Deverell, Garry Worete, *Gondwana Theology: A Trawloolway man reflects on Christian Faith* (Melbourne: Morning Star, 2018).

Deverell, Garry Worete, 'The Bigger Picture: Indigenous theologian Garry Deverell on grounded spirituality', ABC Radio National, 20 September 2020 <https://www.abc.net.au/radionational/programs/soul-search/past-programs/> (accessed 22 September 2020).

Diamond, Jared, *The World until Yesterday: What can we learn from traditional societies?* (London: Penguin, 2013).

Docker, John, *Australian Cultural Elites: Intellectual traditions in Sydney and Melbourne* (Sydney: Angus and Robertson, 1974).

Elder, Bruce, *Blood on the Wattle: Massacres and Maltreatment of Australian Aborigines since 1788* (Sydney: Child & Associates, 1988).

Gammage, Bill, *The Biggest Estate on Earth: How Aborigines made Australia* (Sydney: Allen & Unwin, 2011).

Grant, Stan, *Talking to My Country* (Sydney: HarperCollins, 2017).

Grant, Stan, *On Identity* (Melbourne: MUP, 2019).

Griffiths, Billy, *Deep Time Dreaming: Uncovering Ancient Australia* (Melbourne: Black Inc, 2018).

Habel, Norman, *The Land in Mine: Six Biblical Land Ideologies* (Minneapolis: Fortress, 1995).

Habel, Norman (ed.), *Readings from the Perspective of the Earth* (Sheffield: Sheffield Academic Press, 2000).

Habel, Norman, and Shirley Wurst (eds), *The Earth Story in Genesis: Earth Bible 2* (Sheffield: Sheffield Academic Press, 2000).

Habel, Norman, *An Inconvenient Text: Is a Green Reading of the Bible Possible?* (Adelaide: ATF, 2009).

Habel, Norman 'The Adelaide Declaration on Religion and the Environment', in *Ecotheology*, 5&6 (1998–1999): 255–56.

Harris, John, *We wish we'd done more: Ninety years of CMS and Aboriginal issues in north Australia*, revised edition (Adelaide: Openbook, 1998),

Harrison, Peter, *The Territories of Science and Religion* (Chicago and London: University of Chicago Press, 2015).

Heiss, Anita (ed.) *Growing up Aboriginal in Australia* (Melbourne: Black Inc, 2018).

Hofstede, Geert, https://geerthofstede.com/culture-geert-hofstede-gert-jan-hofstede/6d-model-of-national-culture/ (accessed 6 July 2020).

Hofstede, Geert, 'Dimensionalizing Cultures: The Hofstede Model in Context. Online Readings in Psychology and Culture, Unit 2' (2011). (Retrieved from http://scholarworks.gvsu.edu/orpc/vol2/iss1/8, 17 August 2020).

Korff, Jens <https://www.creativespirits.info/aboriginalculture/history/australian-aboriginal-history-timeline/massacres> (accessed 4 July 2020).

Kwaymullina, Ambelin, *Living on Stolen Land* (Broome: Magabala, 2020).

Lindbeck, George, *The Nature of Doctrine: Religion and Theology in a Post-Liberal Age* (London: SPCK, 1984).

Link-Wieczorek, Ulrike (ed.) *Gastlichkeit: Eine Herausforfderung für Theologie, Kirche und Gesellschaft* (Leipzig: Evangelische Verlagsanstalt, 2018).

Loughrey, Glenn, *Another Time, Another Place: Towards an Australian Church* (Melbourne: Coventry, 2019).

Loughrey, Glenn, *On Being Blackfella's Young Fella: Is Being Aboriginal Enough?* (Melbourne: Coventry, 2020).

Macintyre, Stuart, and Anna Clark, *The History Wars* (Melbourne: MUP, 2003).

McKenna, Mark, *Moment of Truth. Quarterly Essay 69* (Melbourne: Black Inc, 2018).

Maddison, Sarah, *The Colonial Fantasy: Why white Australia can't solve black problems* (Sydney: Allen & Unwin, 2019).

Maddox, Marion, 'How Late Night Theology Sparked a Royal Commission,' in *Sophia: International Journal of Philosophical Theology and Cross Cultural Philosophy of Religion*, 36, 2 (1997): 111–135.

Maddox, Marion, 'What is a "fabrication": The Political Status of Religious Belief,' in *Australian Religion Studies Review*, 11, 1 (1998): 5–16.

Maddox, Marion, 'Religious Belief in the Hindmarsh Island Controversy,' in George Couvalis, Helen Macdonald, and Cheryl Simpson (eds), *Cultural Heritage: Values and Rights* (Adelaide: Proceedings of the 1996 International Conference on Cultural Heritage, Centre for Applied Philosophy, Flinders University, 3–4 October 1996), 61–79. Also at https://mq.academia.edu/MarionMaddox (accessed 5 July 2020).

Marks, Russell, <https://www.themonthly.com.au/blog/russell-marks/2020/05/2020/1580868886/taking-sides-over-dark-emu#mtr> (accessed 23 August 2020).

Milbank, John, Graham Ward, and Catherine Pickstock (eds), *Radical Orthodoxy: A new theology* (Routledge: London/New York, 1999).

Moltmann, Jürgen, *Trinity and the Kingdom of God: The Doctrine of God* (London: SCM Press, 1981).

Moriarty, Ros, *Listening to Country: A journey to the heart of what it means to belong* (Sydney: Allen & Unwin, 2011).

National Constitutional Convention 2017 <https://www.referendumcouncil.org.au/sites/default/files/2017-05/Uluru_Statement_From_The_Heart_0.PDF> (accessed 5 July 2020).

Pascoe, Bruce, *Dark Emu: Aboriginal Australia and the Birth of Agriculture* (Broome: Magabala Books, 2018).

Pascoe, Bruce, *Salt: Selected Stories and Essays* (Melbourne: Black Inc, 2019).

Pascoe, Bruce, 'Andrew Bolt's disappointment,' in *Griffith Review*, 36, https://www.griffithreview.com/editions/what-is-australia-for/ (accessed 19 October 2020).

Pattel-Gray, Anne, *The Great White Flood: Racism in Australia*. American Academy of Religion Cultural Criticism Series, No. 2 (Atlanta: Scholars Press, 1998).

Porter, Muriel, *Land of the Spirit? The Australian Religious Experience* (Geneva: WCC/Melbourne: JBCE, 1990).

Prothero, Stephen, *God is not One: The eight rival religions that run the world & why their differences matter* (Melbourne: Black Inc, 2010).

Raheb, Mitri, *Faith in the Face of Empire: The Bible through Palestinian Eyes* (Bethlehem: Diyar, 2014).

Riches, Tanya, Editorial, in *Australasian Pentecostal Studies* 20, 2019, 4–17.

Rigby, Kate, *Topologies of the Sacred: The Poetics of Place in European Romanticism* (Charlottesville and London: Univ of Virginia Press, 2004).

Ritschl, Dietrich, *Memory and Hope: An inquiry concerning the presence of Christ* (New York: Macmillan, 1967).

Ritschl, Dietrich, *The Logic of Theology: A brief account of the relationships between basic concepts in theology*, tr. John Bowden (Philadelphia: Fortress, 1987).

Rutherford, Adam, *How to Argue with a Racist: History, Science, Race and Reality* (London: Weidenfeld & Nicholson, 2020).

Ryan, Lyndall, https://c21ch.newcastle.edu.au/colonialmassacres/ (accessed 4 April 2020).

Steffensen, Victor, *Fire Country* (Melbourne: Hardie Grant, 2020).

Stockton, Eugene, *The Aboriginal Gift: Spirituality for a Nation* (Sydney: Millennium Books, 1995).

Strehlow, TGH, *Central Australian Religion: Personal Monototenism in a Polytotemic Community* (Adelaide: Australian Association for the Study of Religion, 1978).

Swain, Tony, *A Place for Strangers: Towards a History of Australian Aboriginal Being* (Cambridge: Cambridge Univ. Press, 1993).

Tanner, Kathryn, *God and Creation in Christian Theology: Tyranny or Empowerment?* (Oxford: Blackwell, 1988).

Tanner, Kathryn, *Theories of Culture: a new agenda for theology* (Minneapolis: Fortress, 1997).

Taylor, Charles, *A Secular Age* (Cambridge MA: Belknap, 2007).

Thorpe, Lidia, 'I'm heartbroken by this colonial violence,' in *The Age*, 29 October 2020, 29.

Wallquist, Calla <https://www.theguardian.com/australia-news/2020/may/30/juukan-gorge-rio-tinto-blasting-of-aboriginal-site-prompts-calls-to-change-antiquated-laws> (accessed 30 July 2020).

Whiteley, Raewynne, 'Church in Public Space,' in Bruce Kaye, Sarah Macneil, and Heather Thomson (eds), *'Wonderful and Confessedly Strange': Australian Essays in Anglican Ecclesiology* (Adelaide: ATF Press, 2006), 379–405.

Yettica-Paulson, Mark, 'Mission in the Great South Land: An Indigenous Perspective,' in Mark Brett and Jione Havea, *Colonial Contexts and Postcolonial Theologies: Storyweaving in the Asia Pacific*, (New York: Palgrave Macmillan, 2014), 249–264.

Yunkaporta, Tyson, *Sand Talk: How Indigenous Thinking Can Save the World* (Melbourne: Text, 2019).

Fiction and Poetry

Birch, Tony, *The White Girl* (Brisbane: UQP, 2019).

Carey, Peter, *A Long Way from Home* (Melbourne: Hamish Hamilton, 2017).

Eliot, TS, *Collected Poems 1909–1962* (London: Faber and Faber, 1963).

Gare, Nene, *The Fringe Dwellers* (Melbourne: Heinemann, 1961).

Grenville, Kate, *The Secret River* (Melbourne: Text, 2005).

Grenville, Kate, *A Room made of Leaves* (Melbourne: Text, 2020).

Janson, Julie, *Benevolence* (Broome: Magabala, 2020).

Melissa Lucashenko's *Too Much Lip* (Brisbane: UQP, 2018).

Miller, Alex, *Journey to the Stone Country* (Sydney: Allen & Unwin, 2003).

Purcell, Leah, *The Drover's Wife* (Sydney: Hamish Hamilton, 2019).

Scott, Kim, *That Deadman Dance* (Sydney: Picador, 2011).

Scott, Kim, *Taboo* (Sydney: Picador, 2017).

Treloar, Lucy, *Salt Creek* (Sydney: Picador, 2015).

White, Patrick, *Voss* (Sydney: Knopf, 2012).

Winch, Tara June, *The Yield* (Melbourne: Hamish Hamilton, 2019).

Winton, Tim, *Cloud Street* (Melbourne: McPhee Gribble, 1991).

Wright, Alexis, *Carpentaria* (Sydney: Giramondo, 2006).

CPSIA information can be obtained
at www.ICGtesting.com
Printed in the USA
BVHW042006291021
620152BV00002B/117